THANK YOU FOR PURCHASING ICE CREAM MADNESS VOLUME 2. IF YOU ENJOYED YOUR COLORING EXPERIENCE, PLEASE CHECK OUT THESE OTHER BOOKS BY ME AT AMAZON.COM:

VINTAGE WINE GARDEN

VINTAGE PARIS BAKE SHOP

ICE CREAM MADNESS

TEA & COFFEE TROPICAL TREASURES

TEA & COFFEE OCEAN TREASURES

TEA & COFFEE TREASURES

BOTANICAL FLOWERS & MANDALAS

MAJESTIC FALL

A VERY RETRO CHRISTMAS

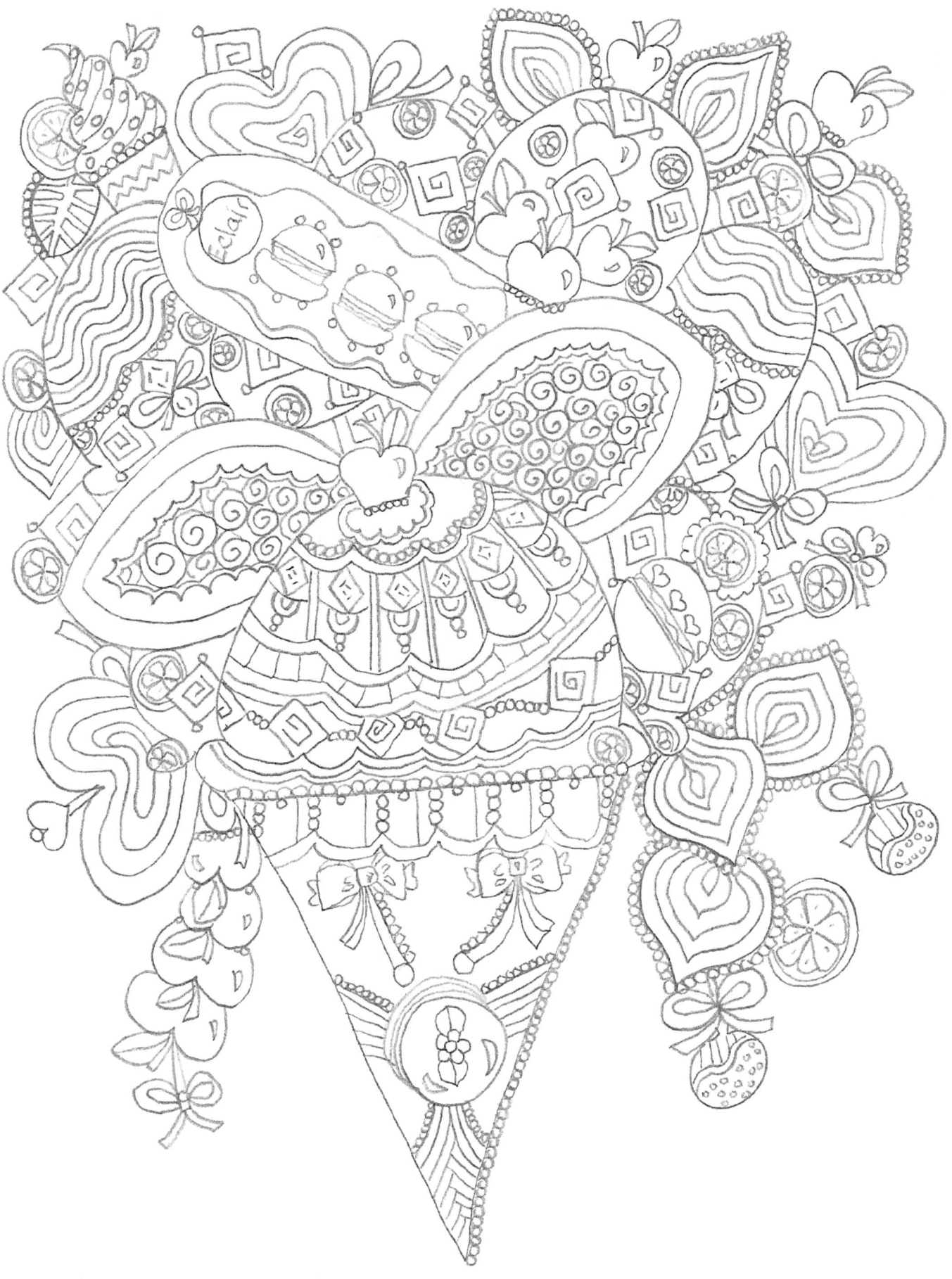

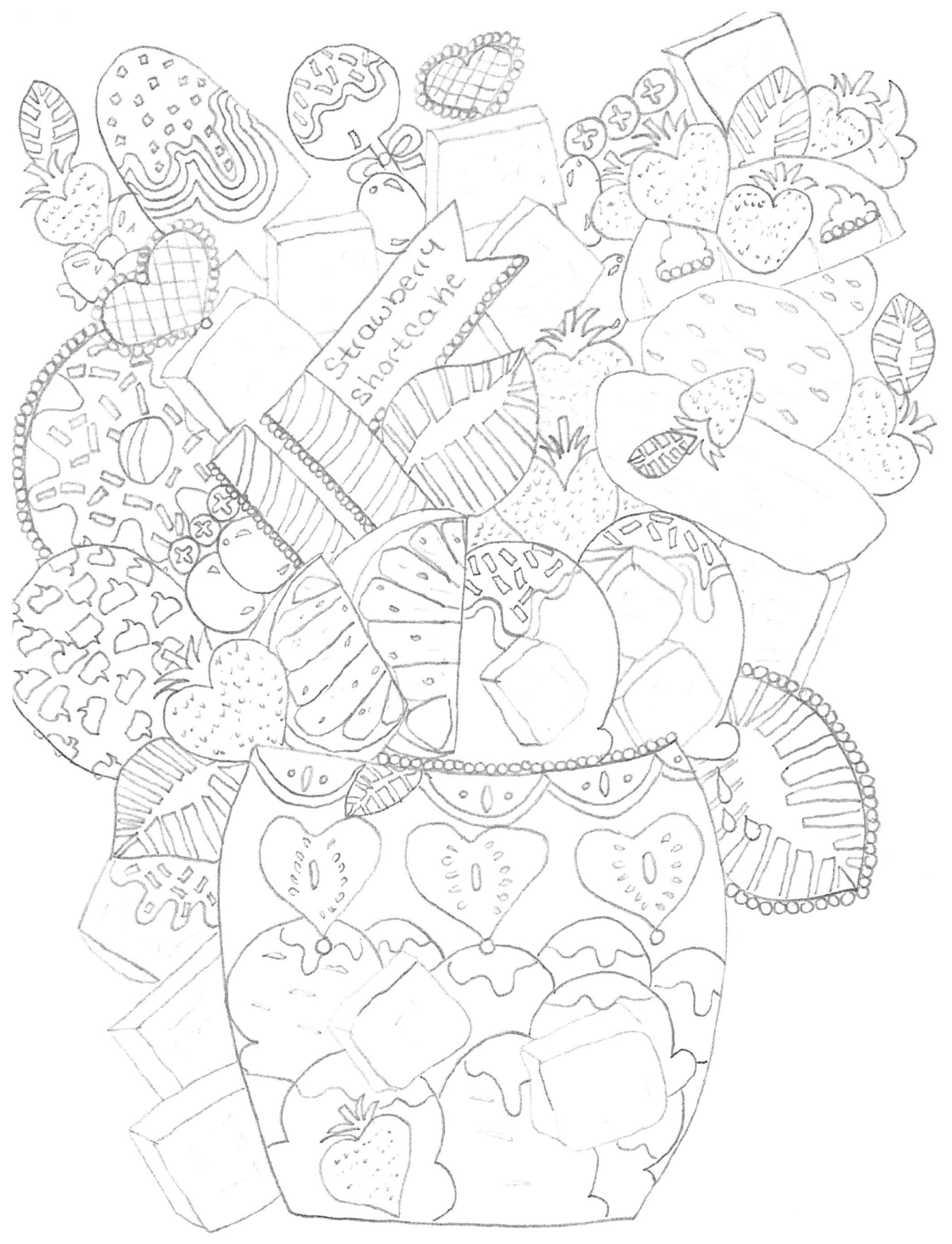

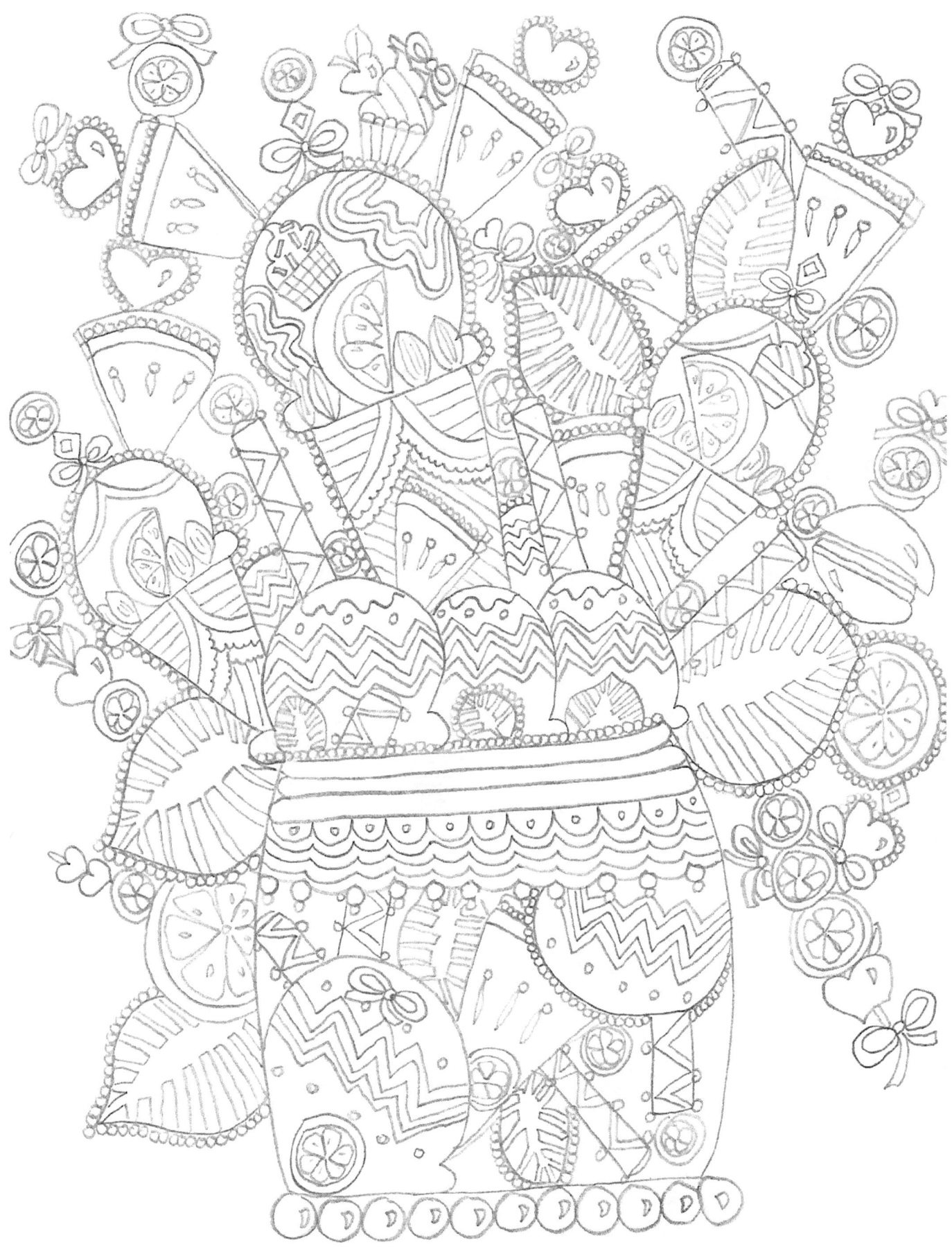

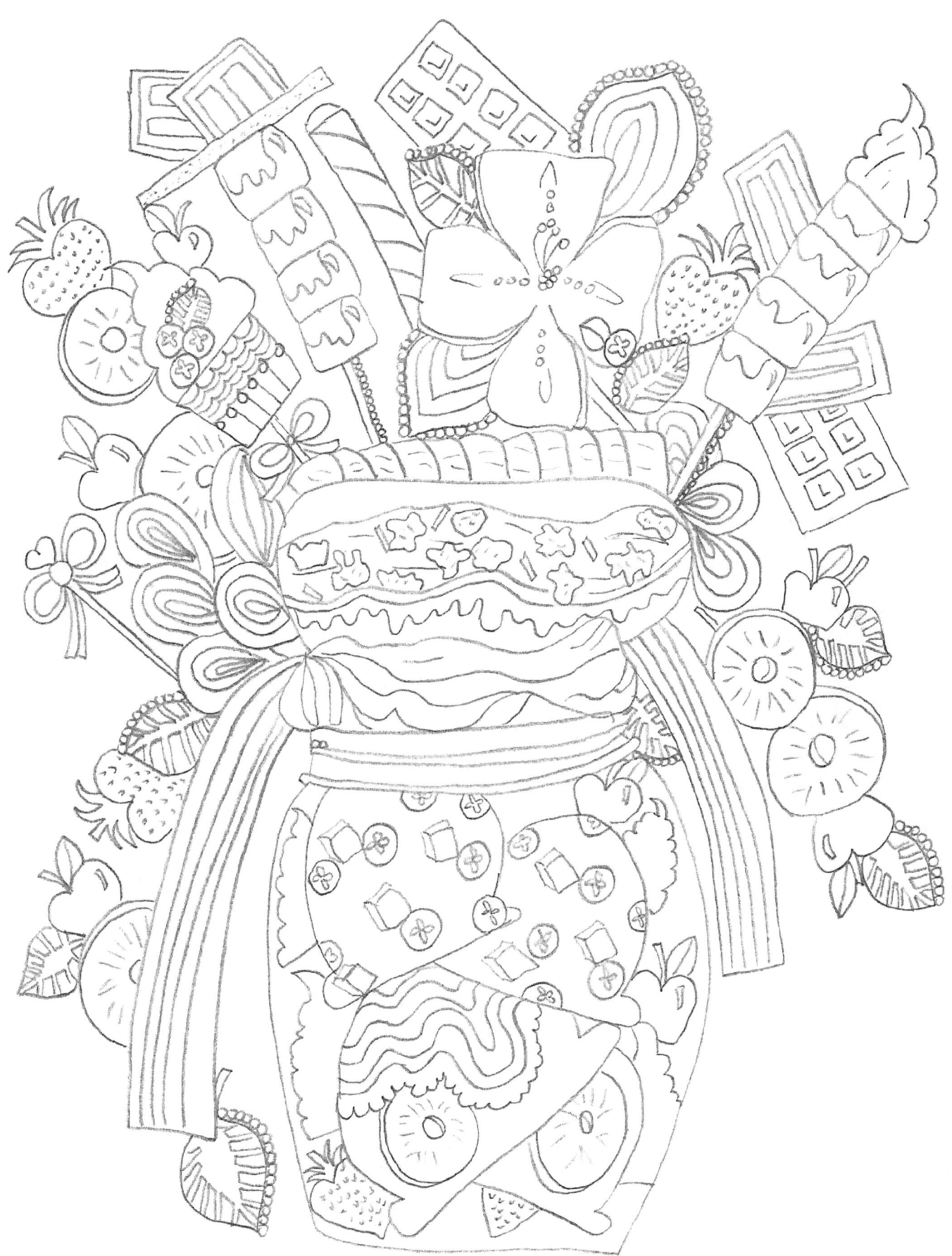

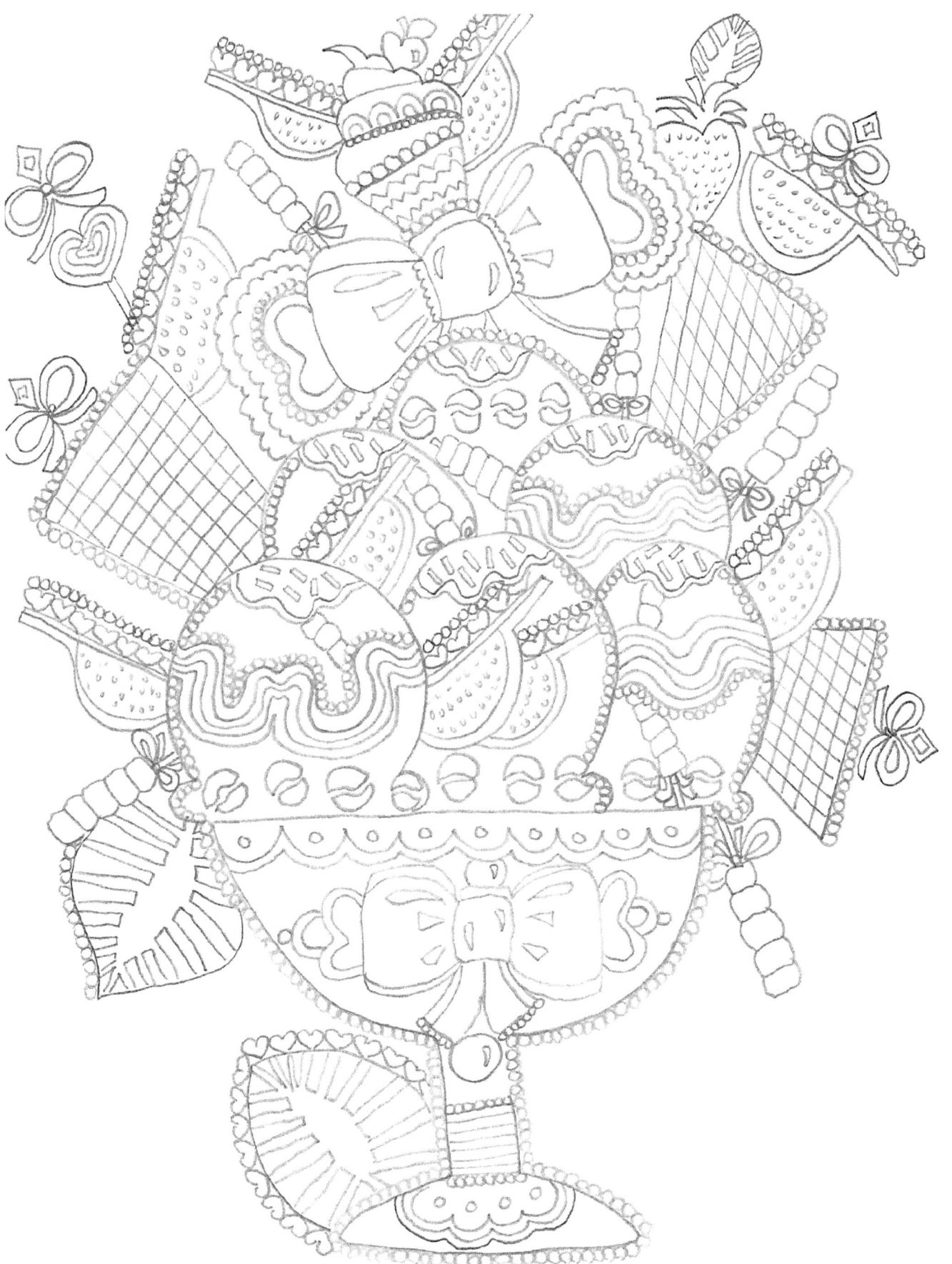

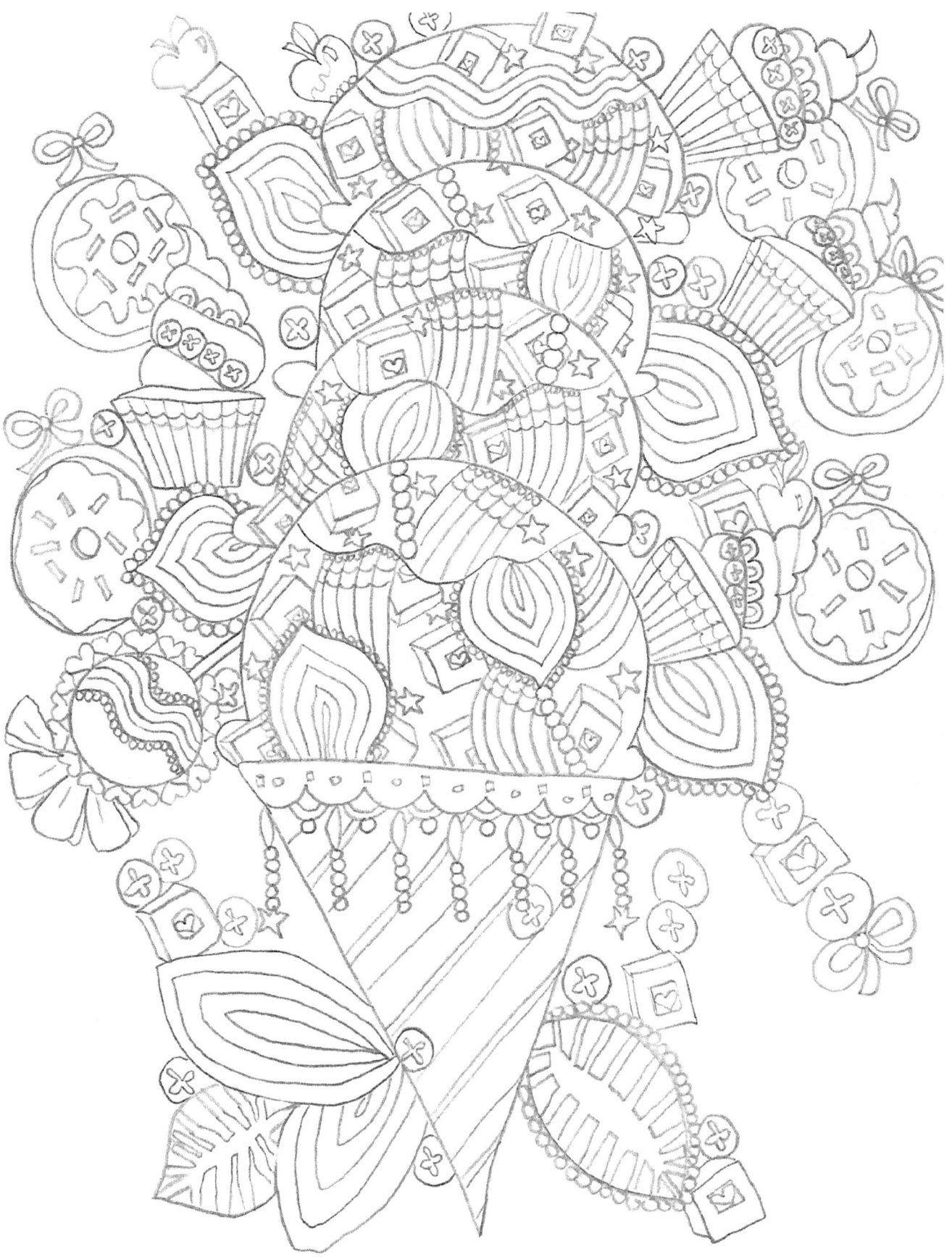

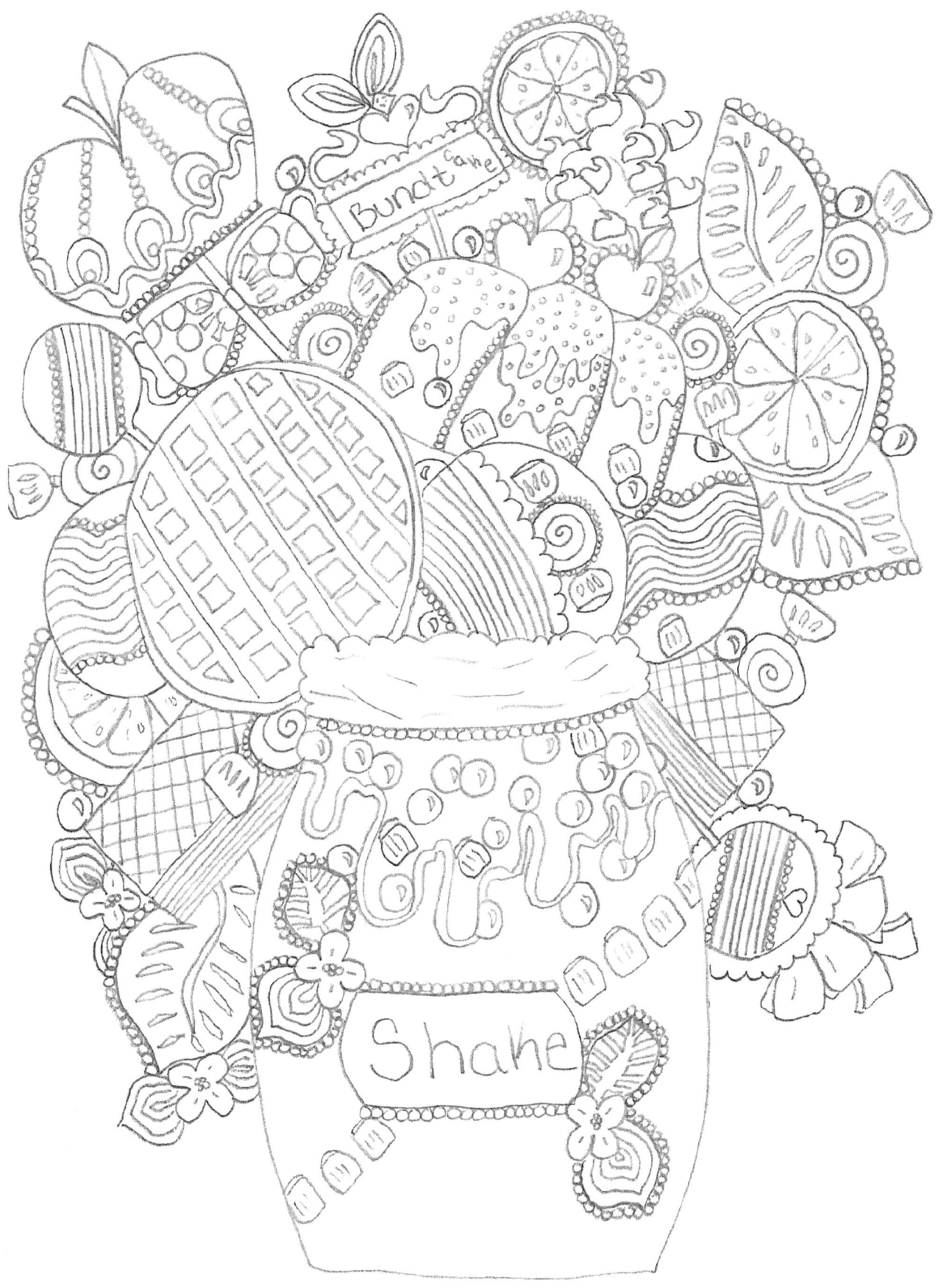

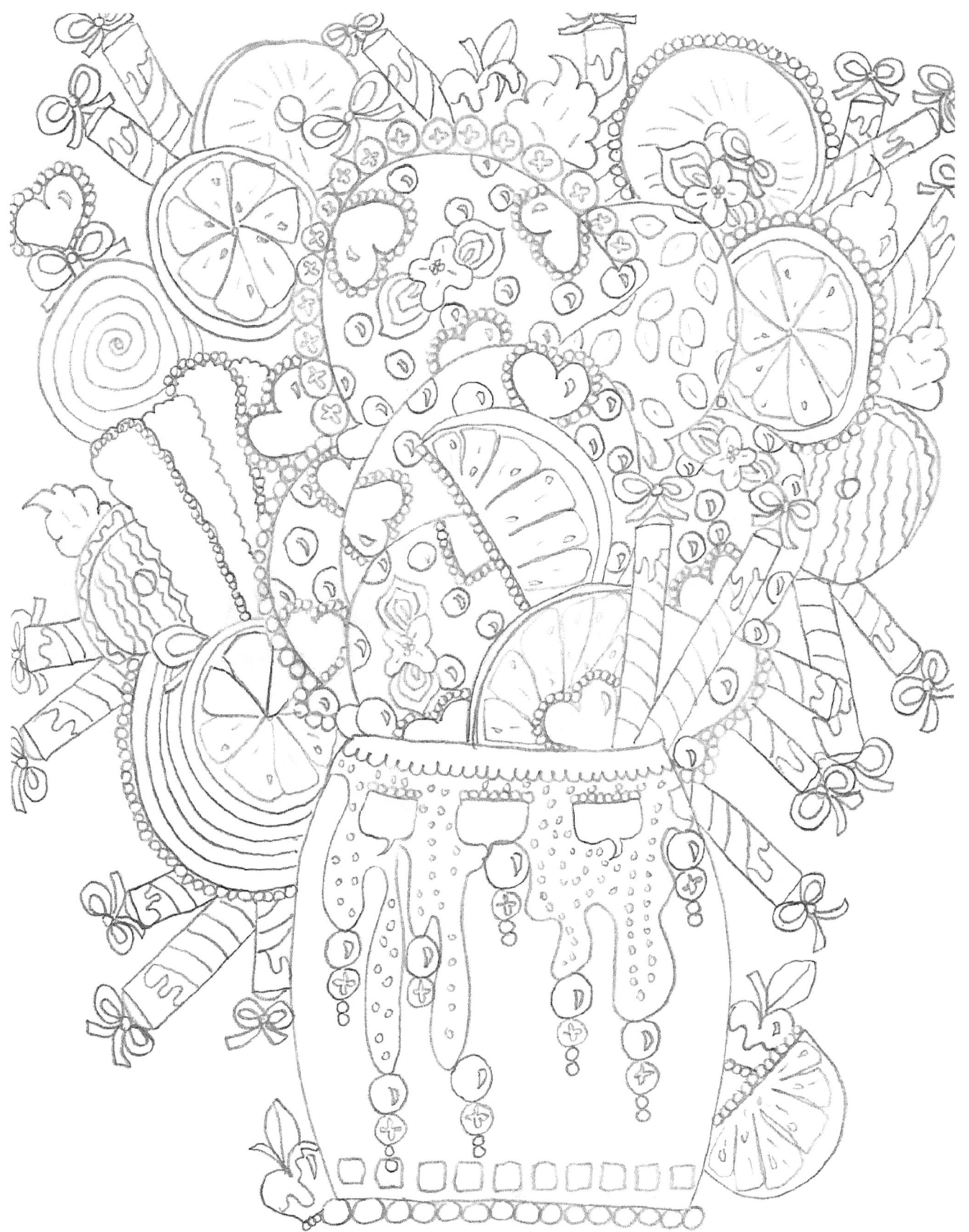

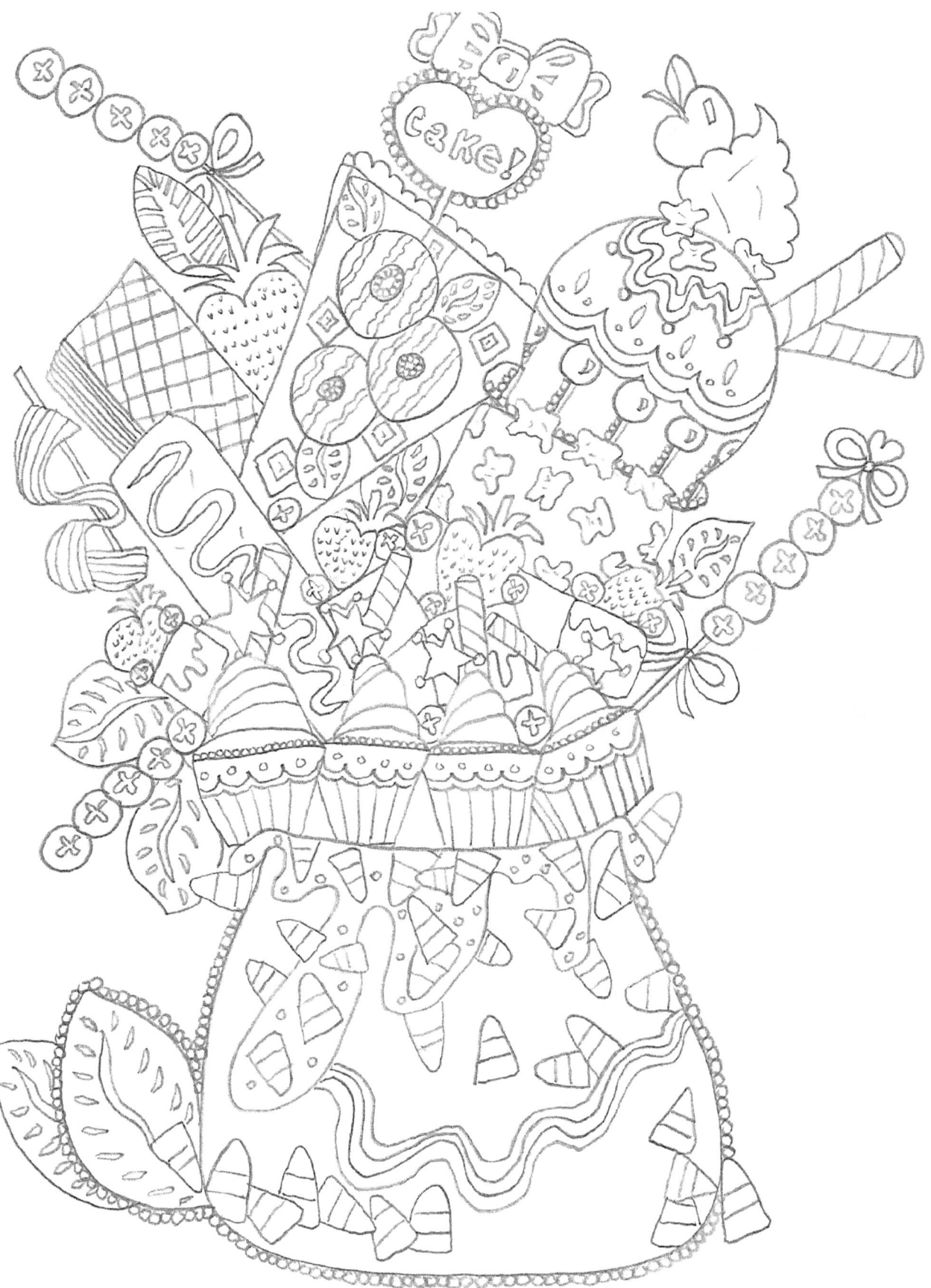

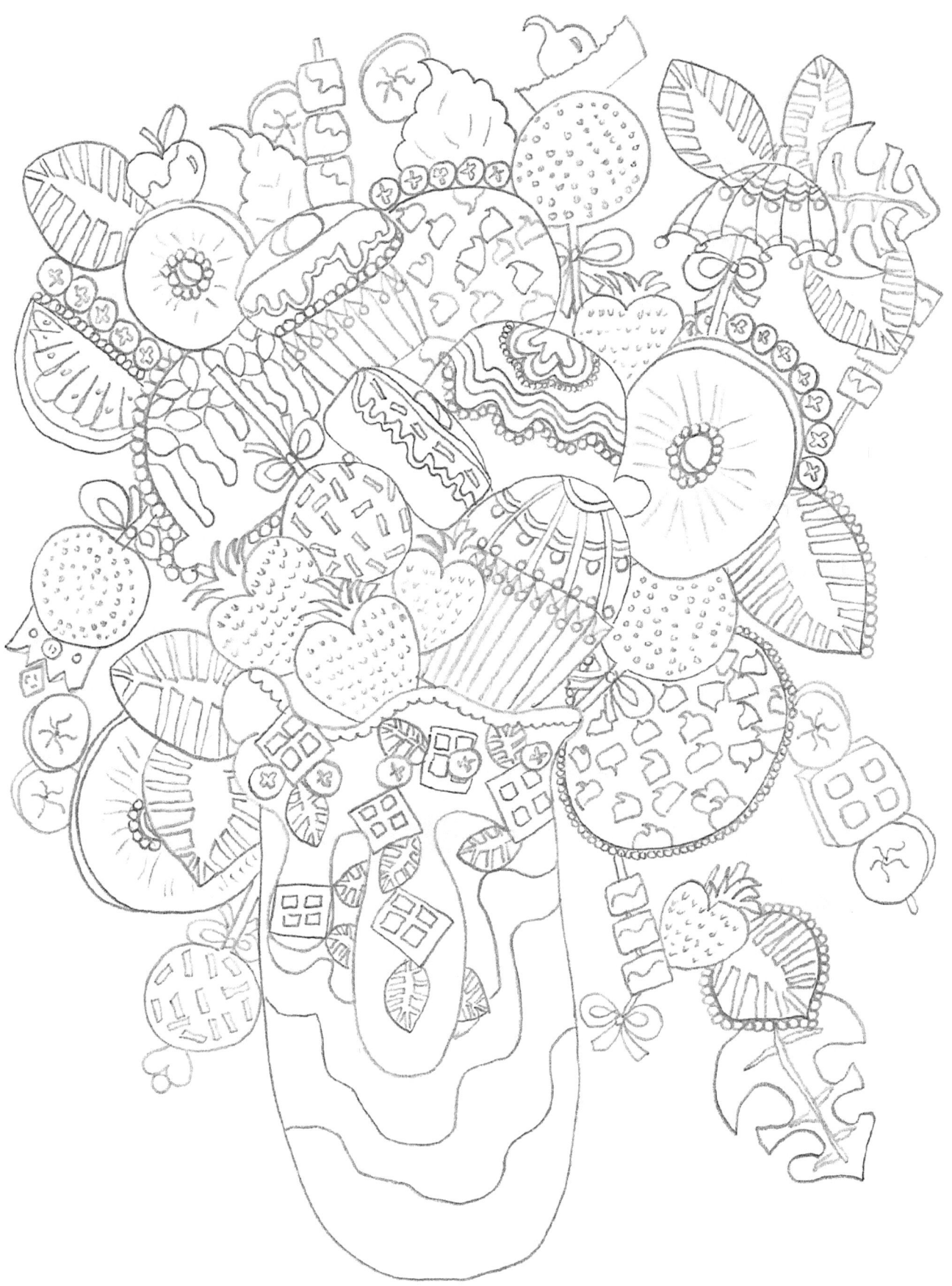

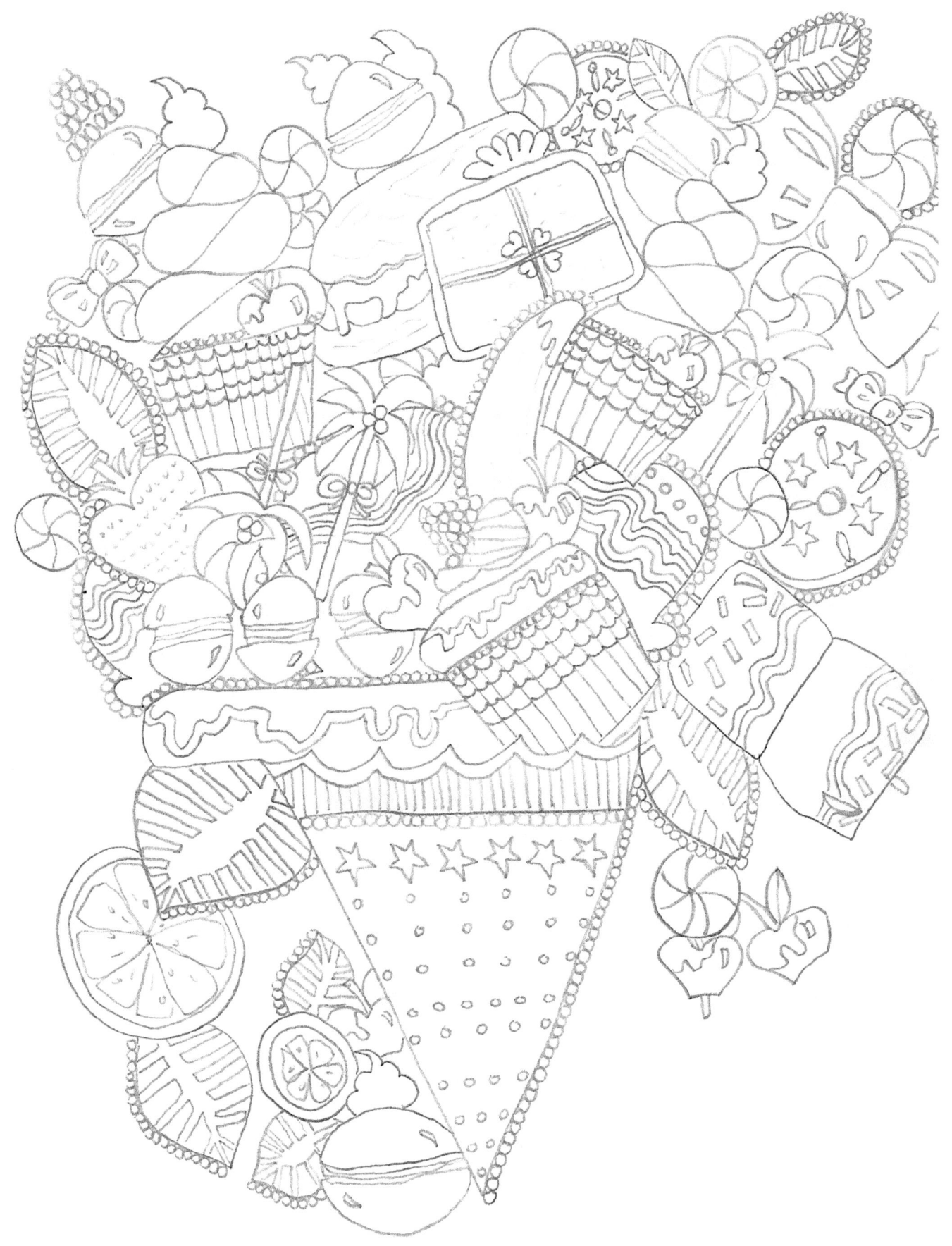

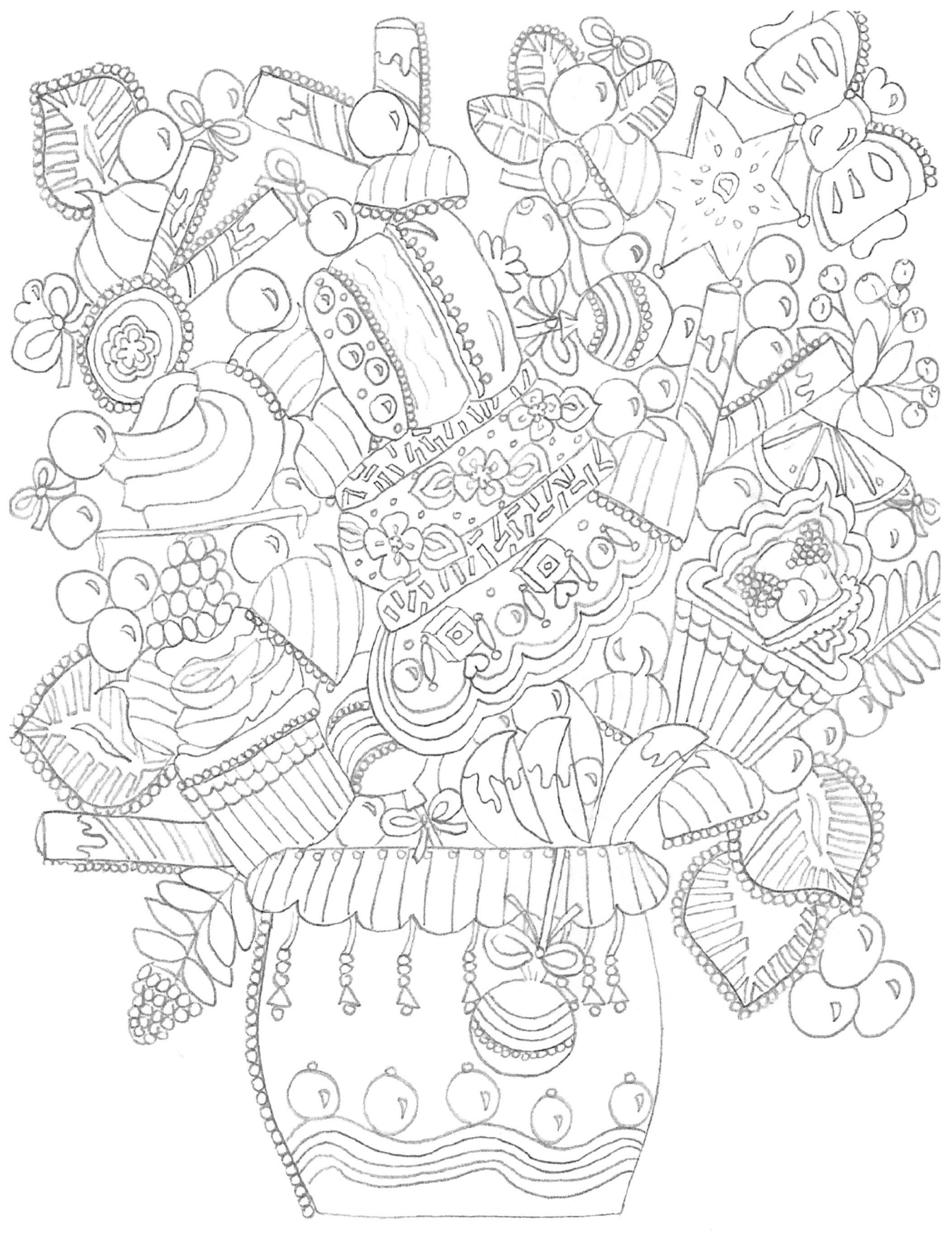

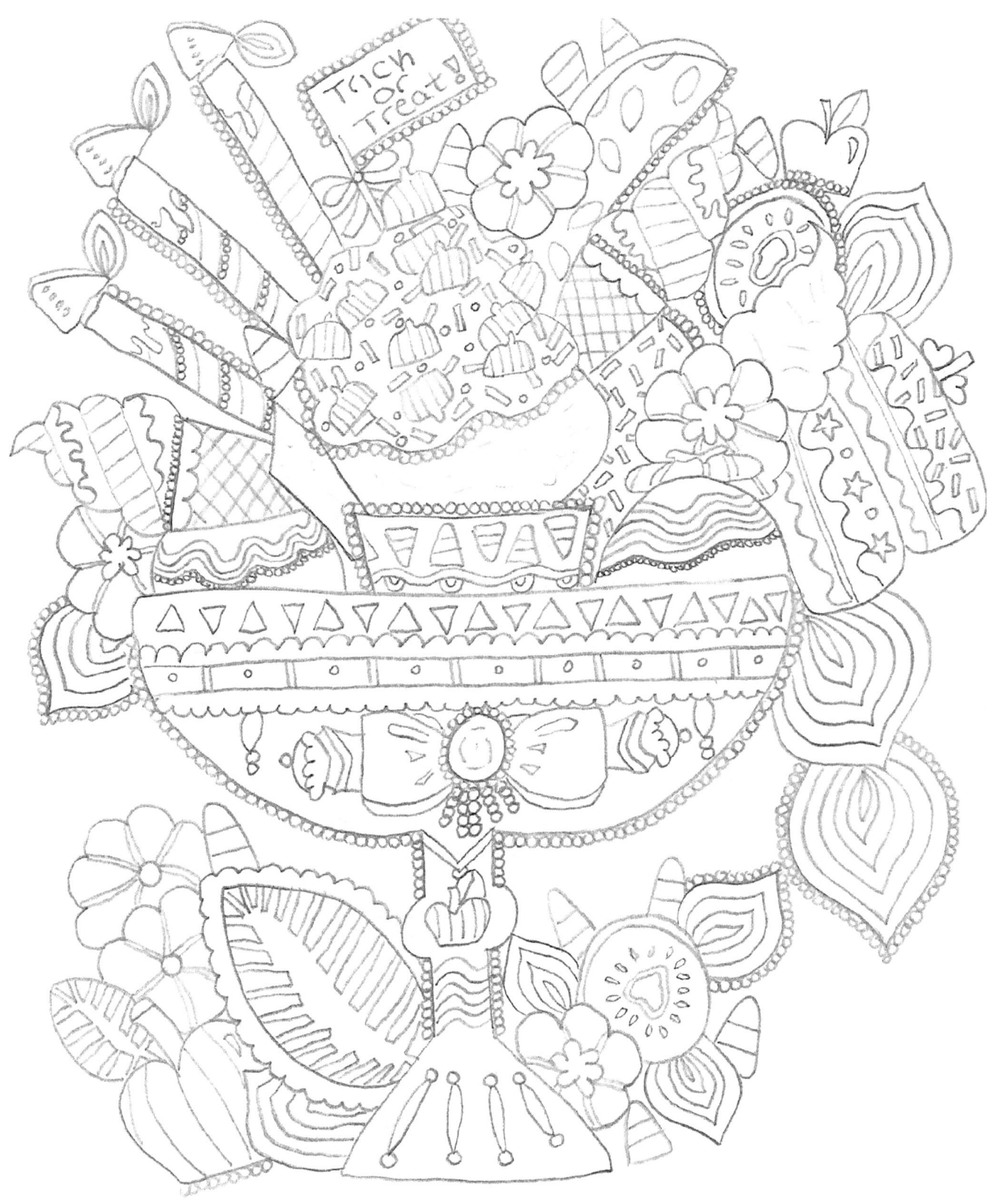

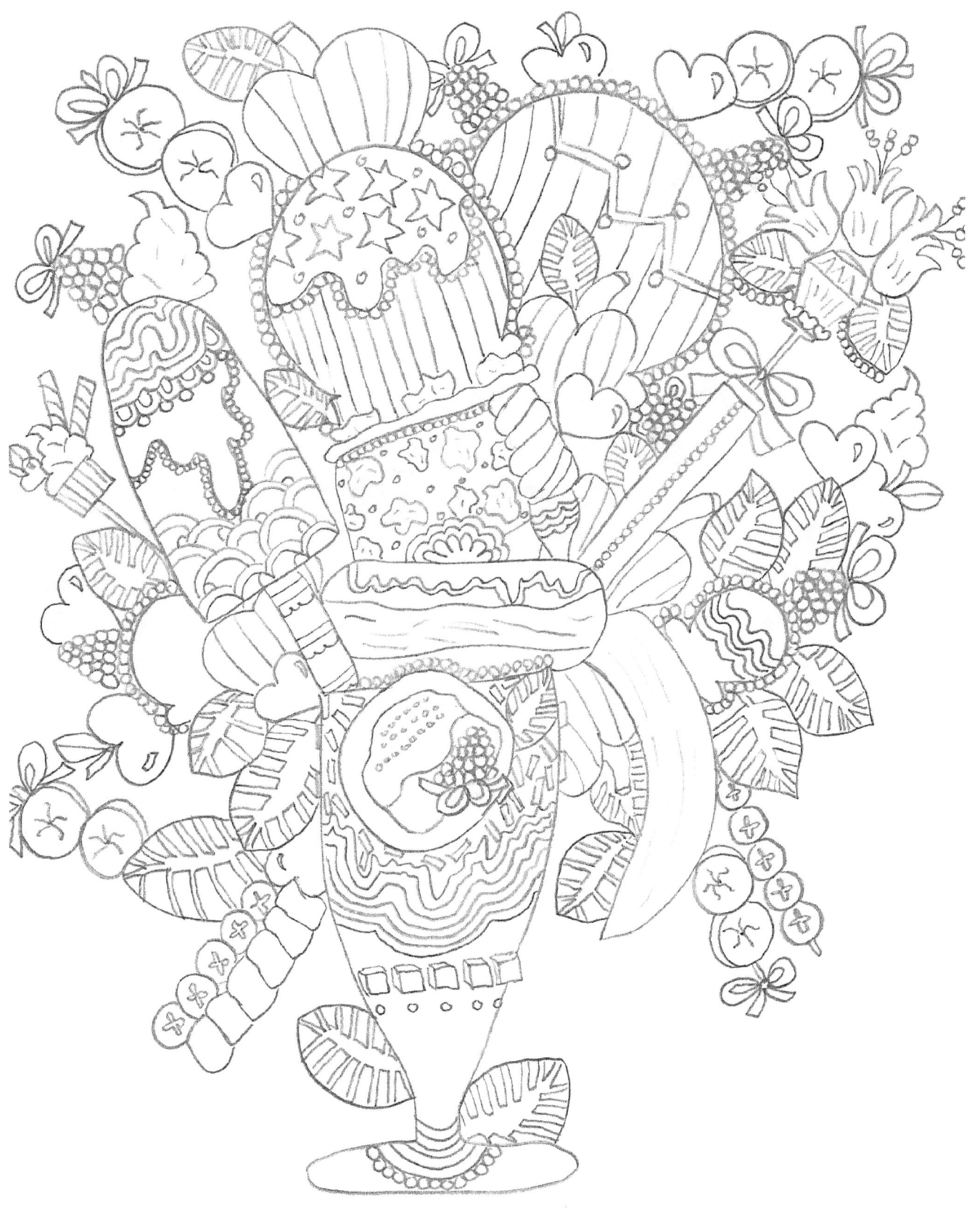

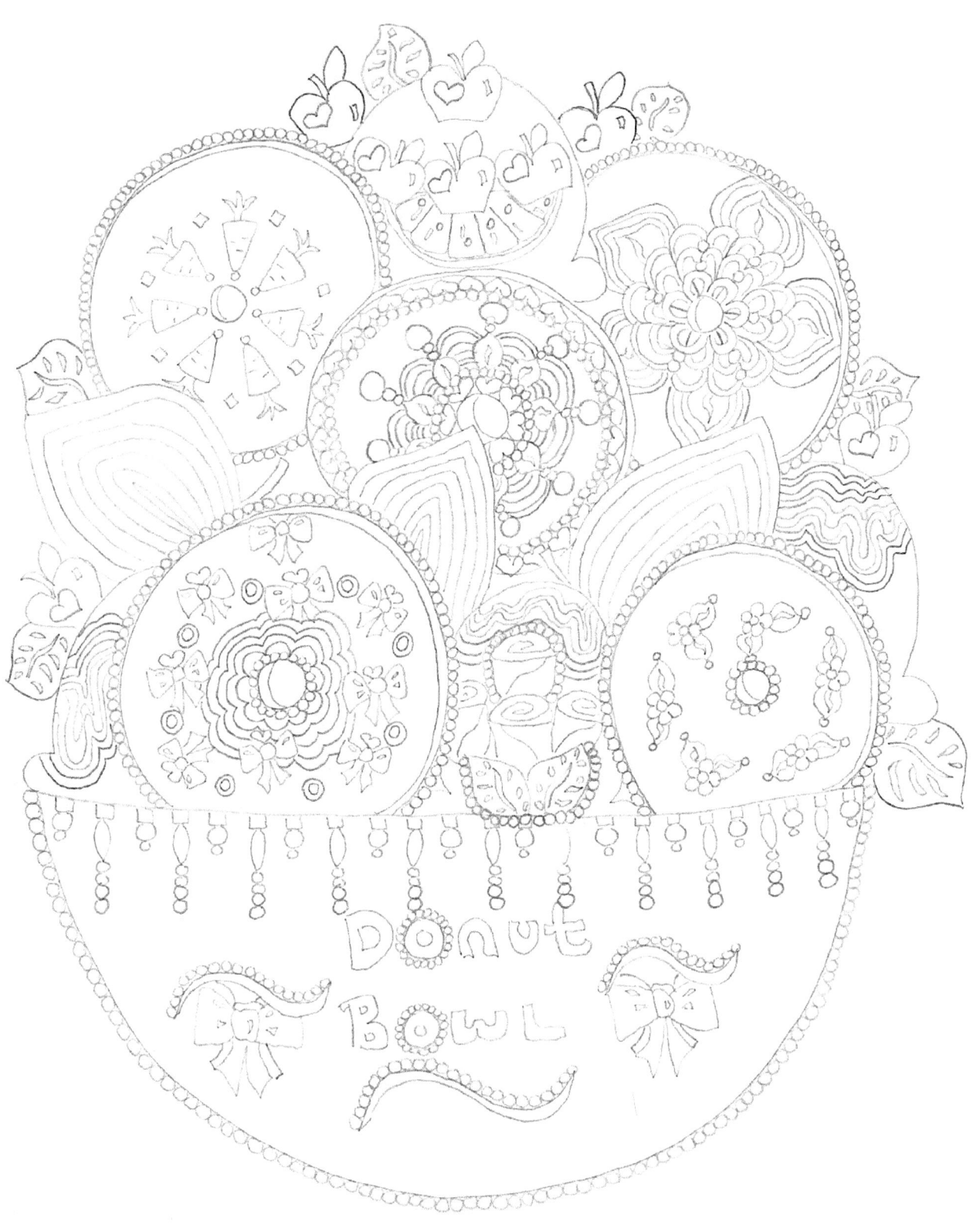

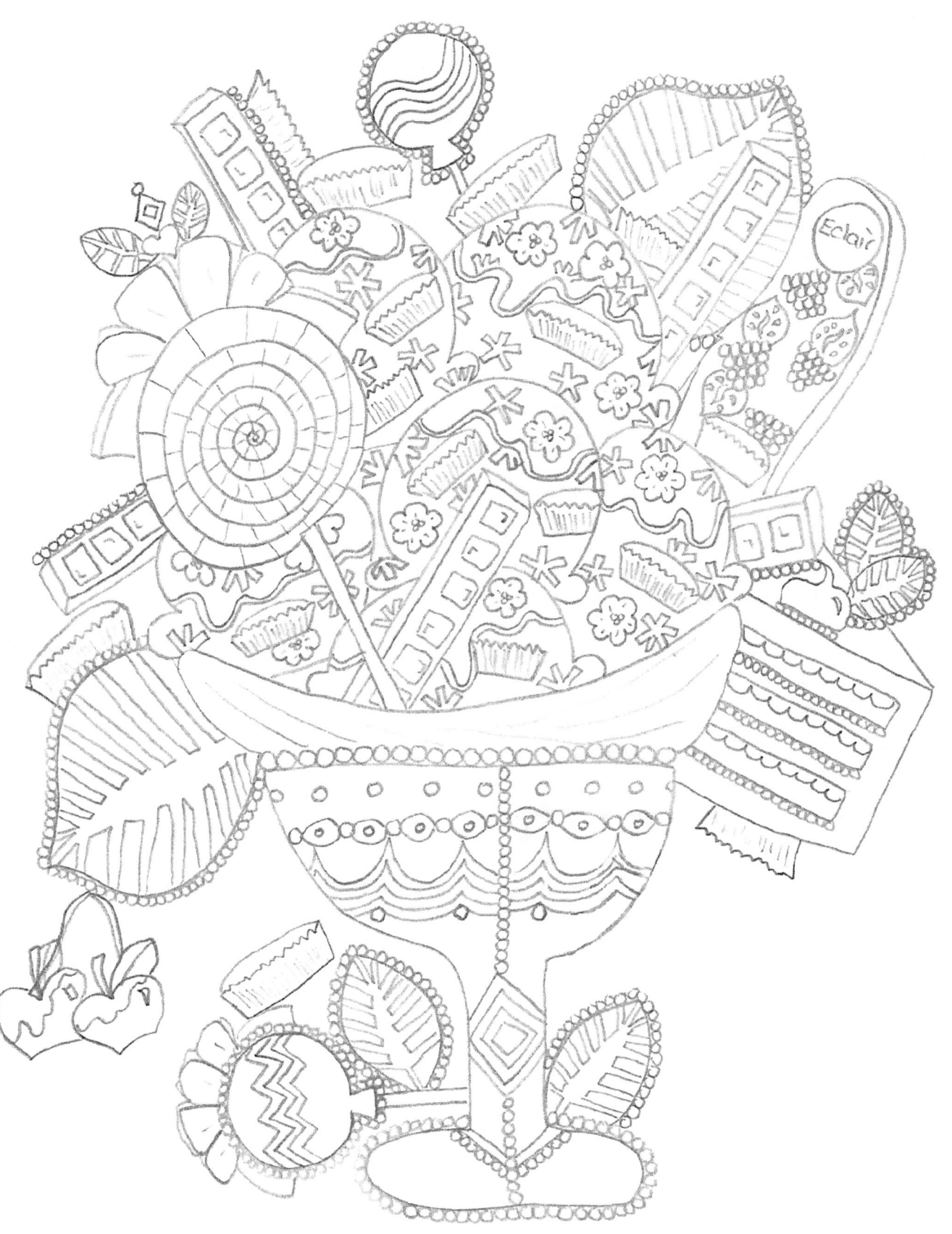

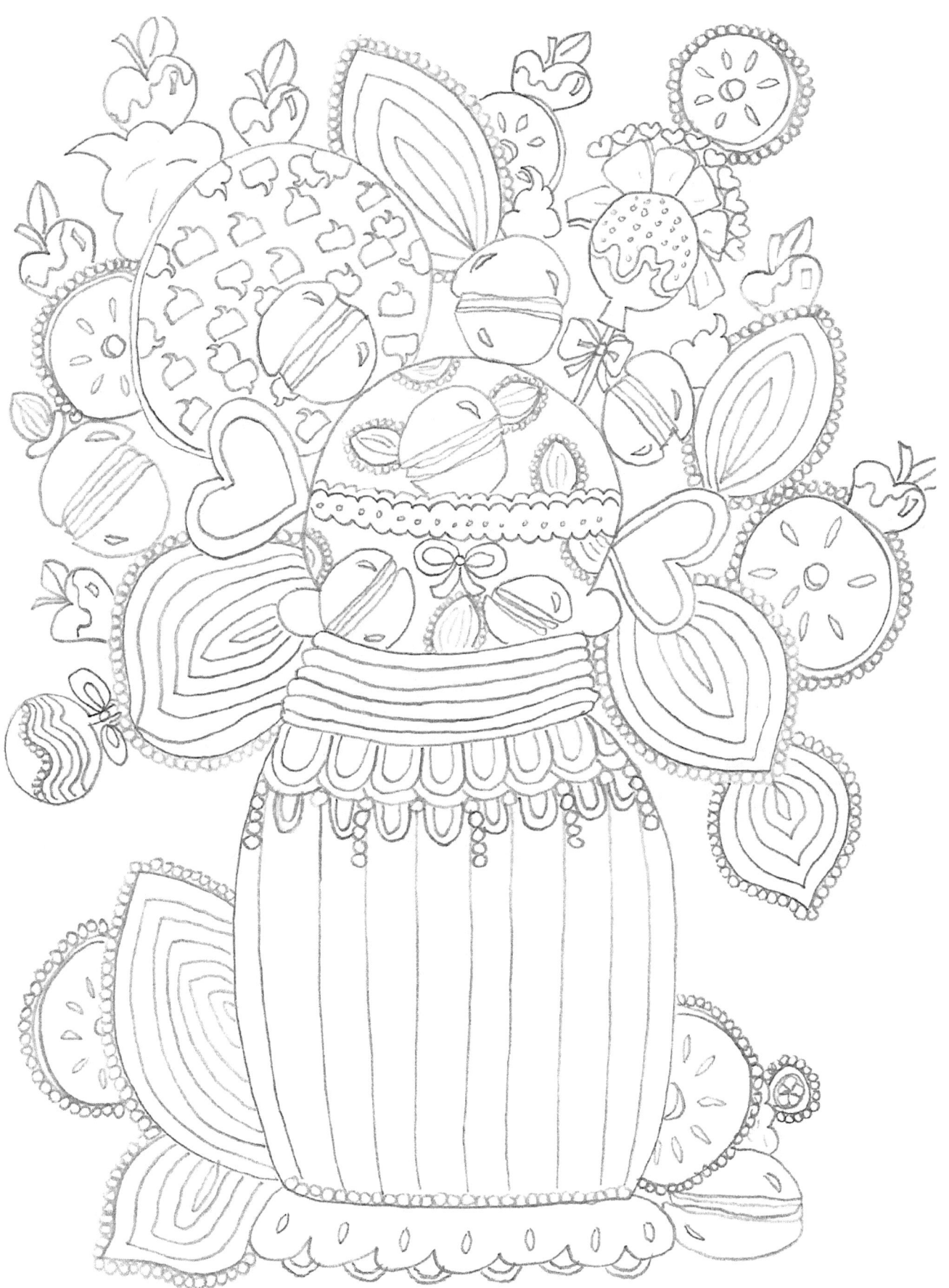

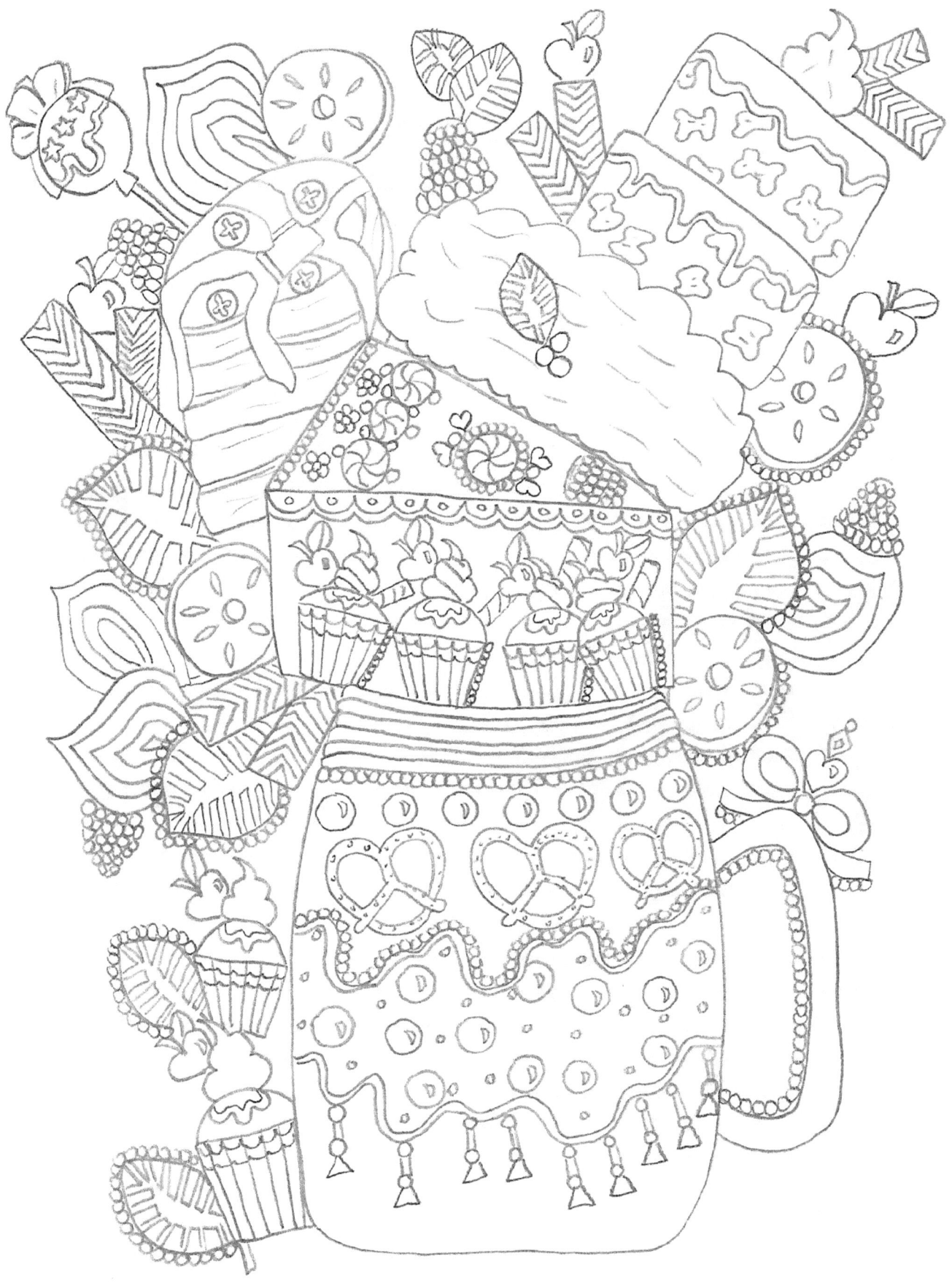

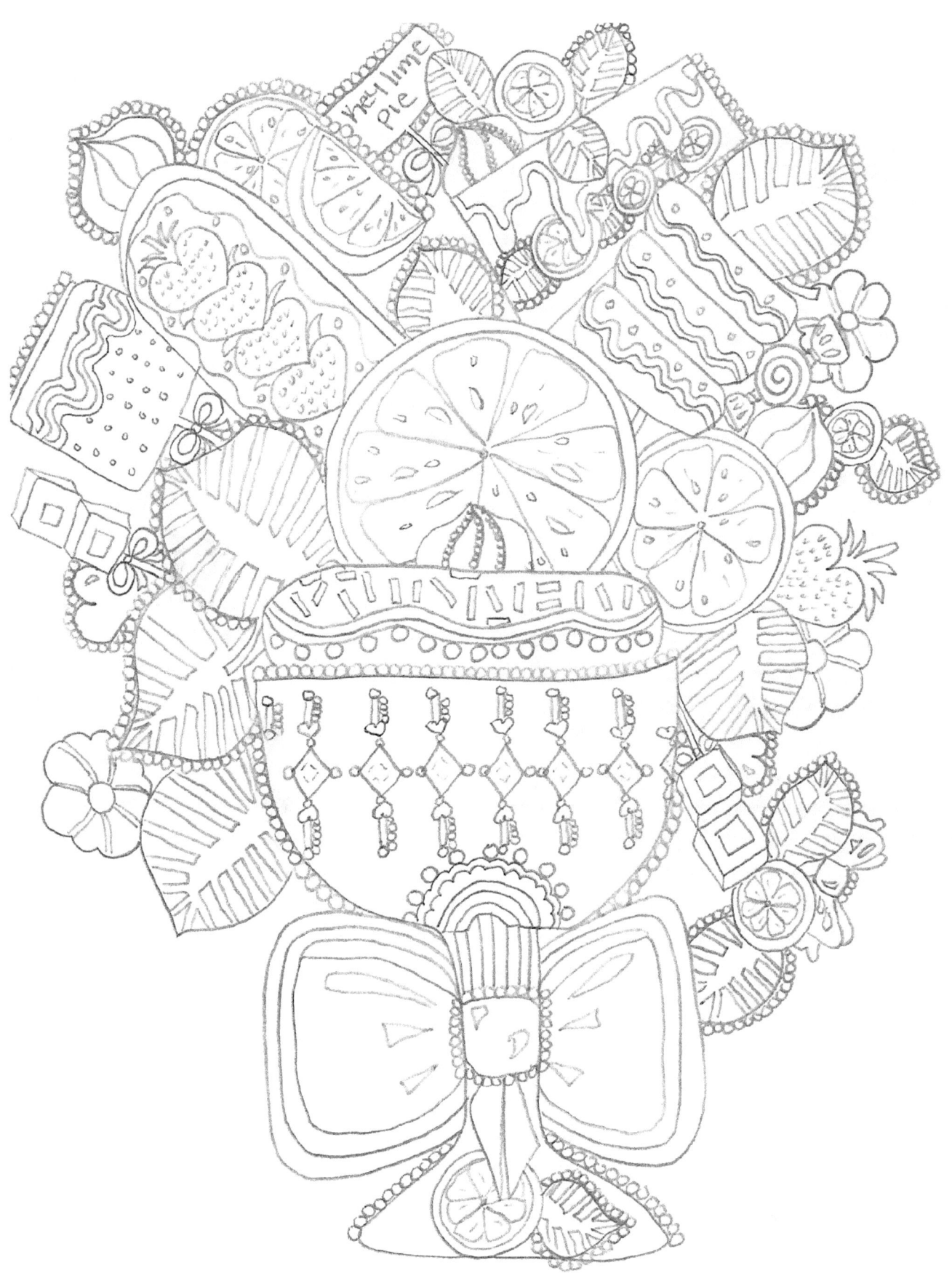

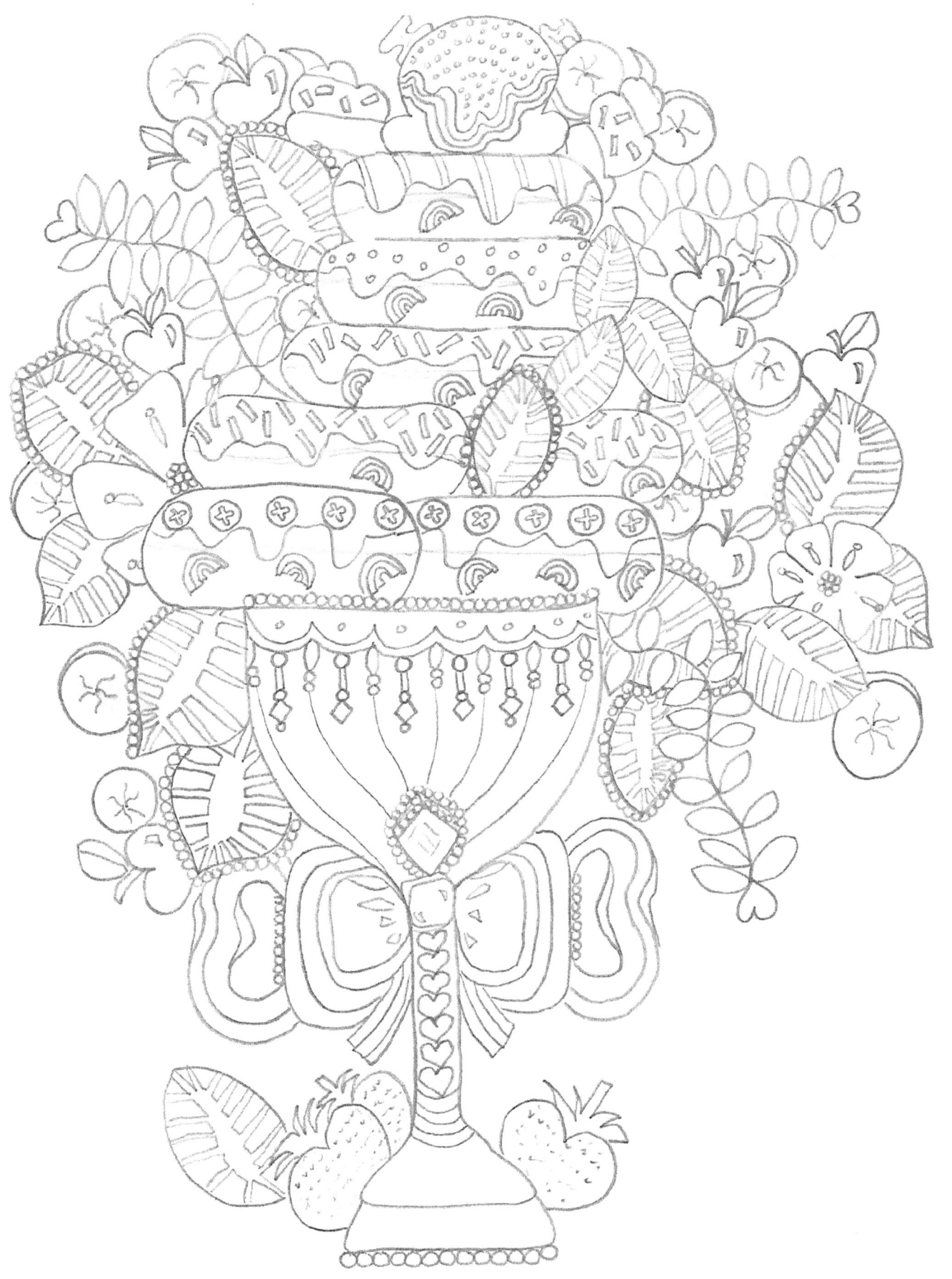

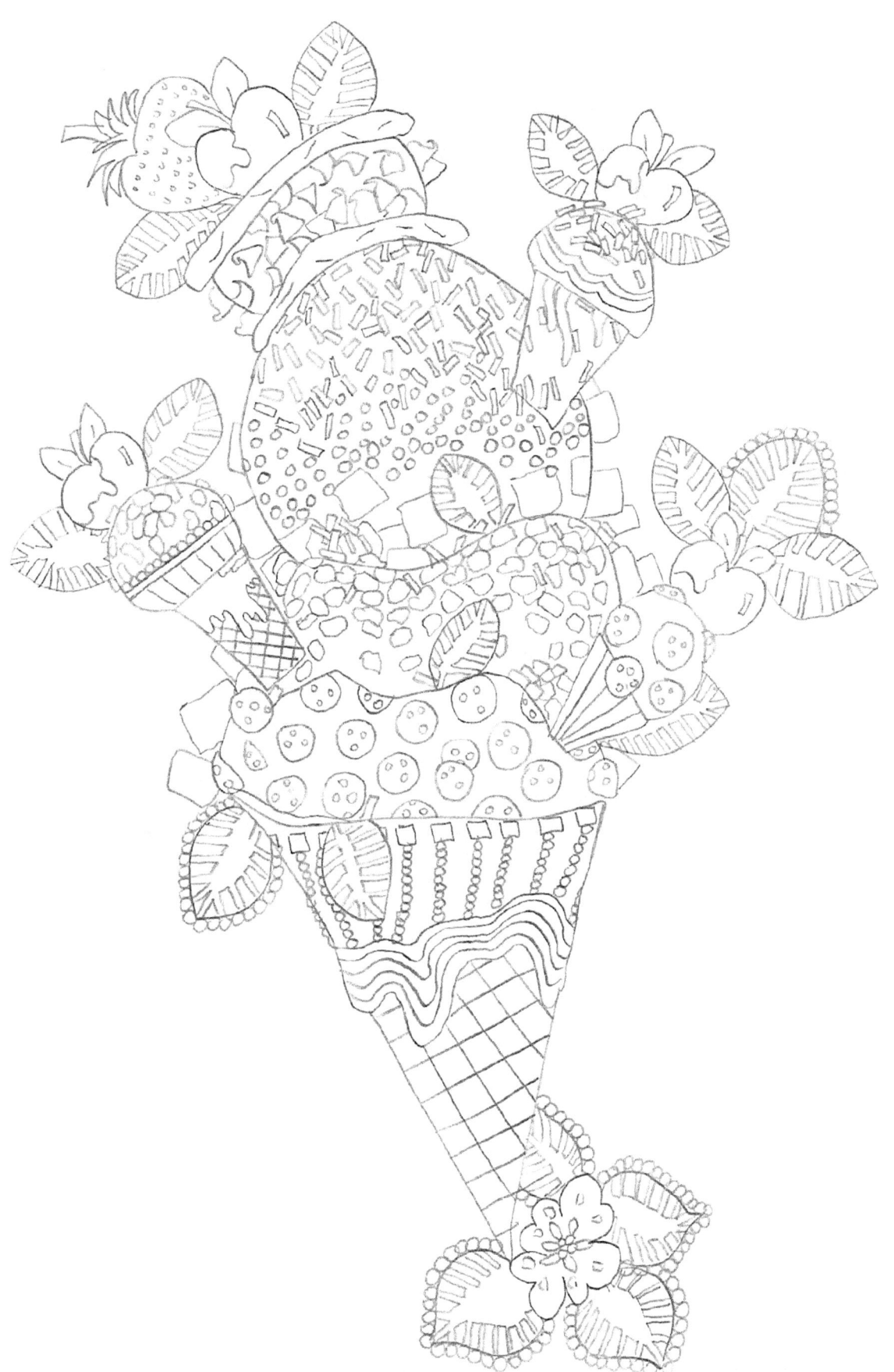

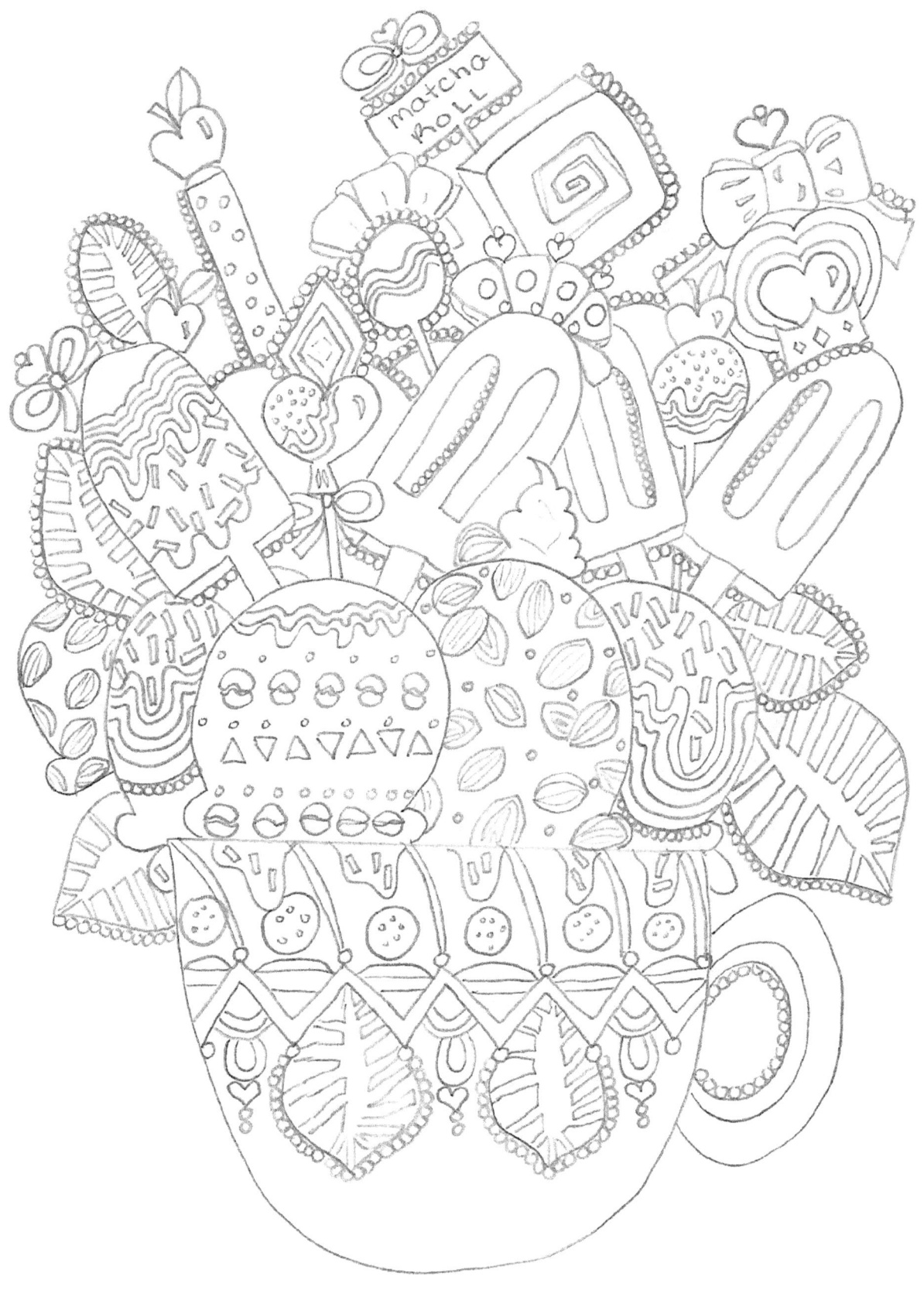

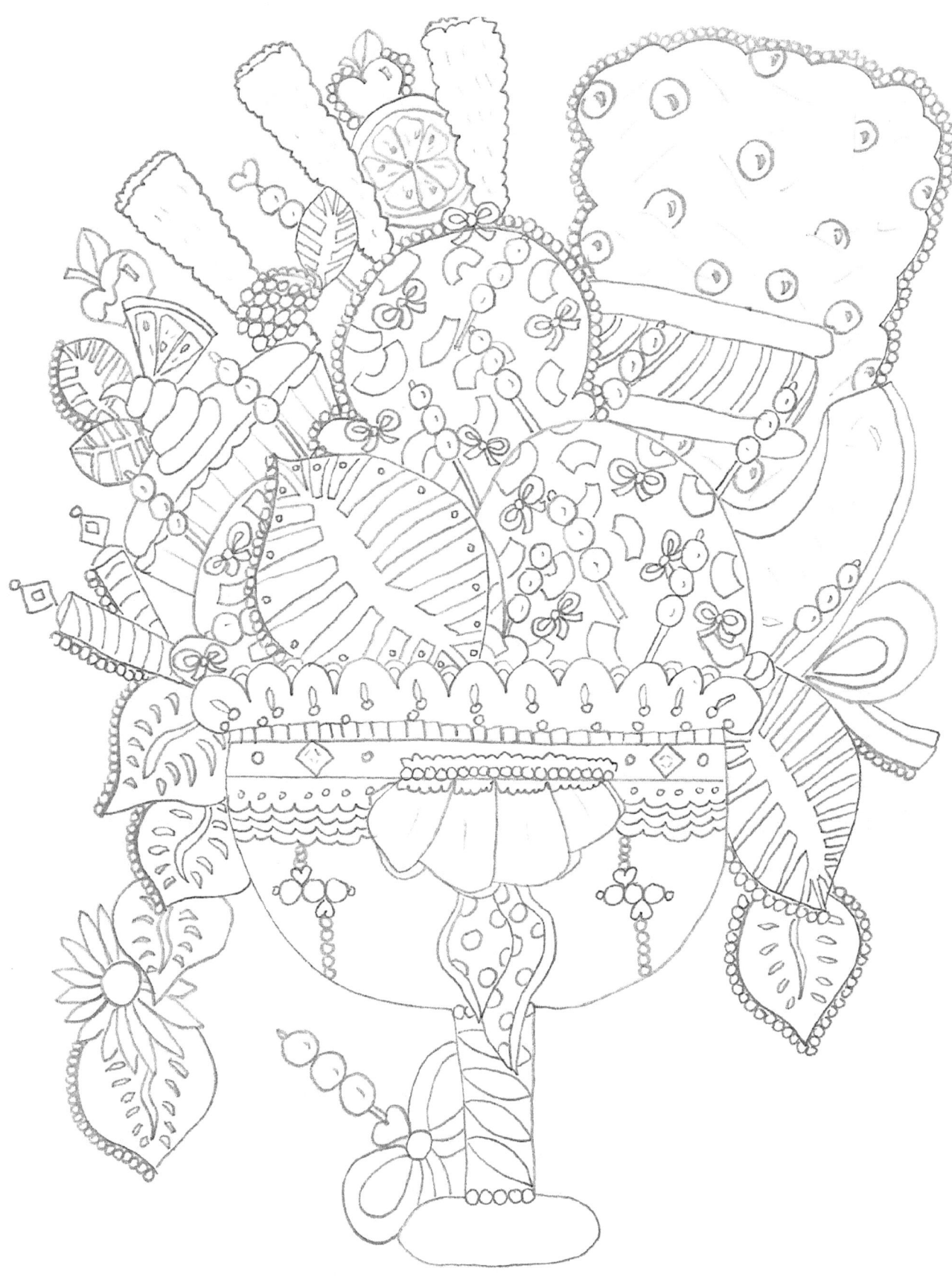

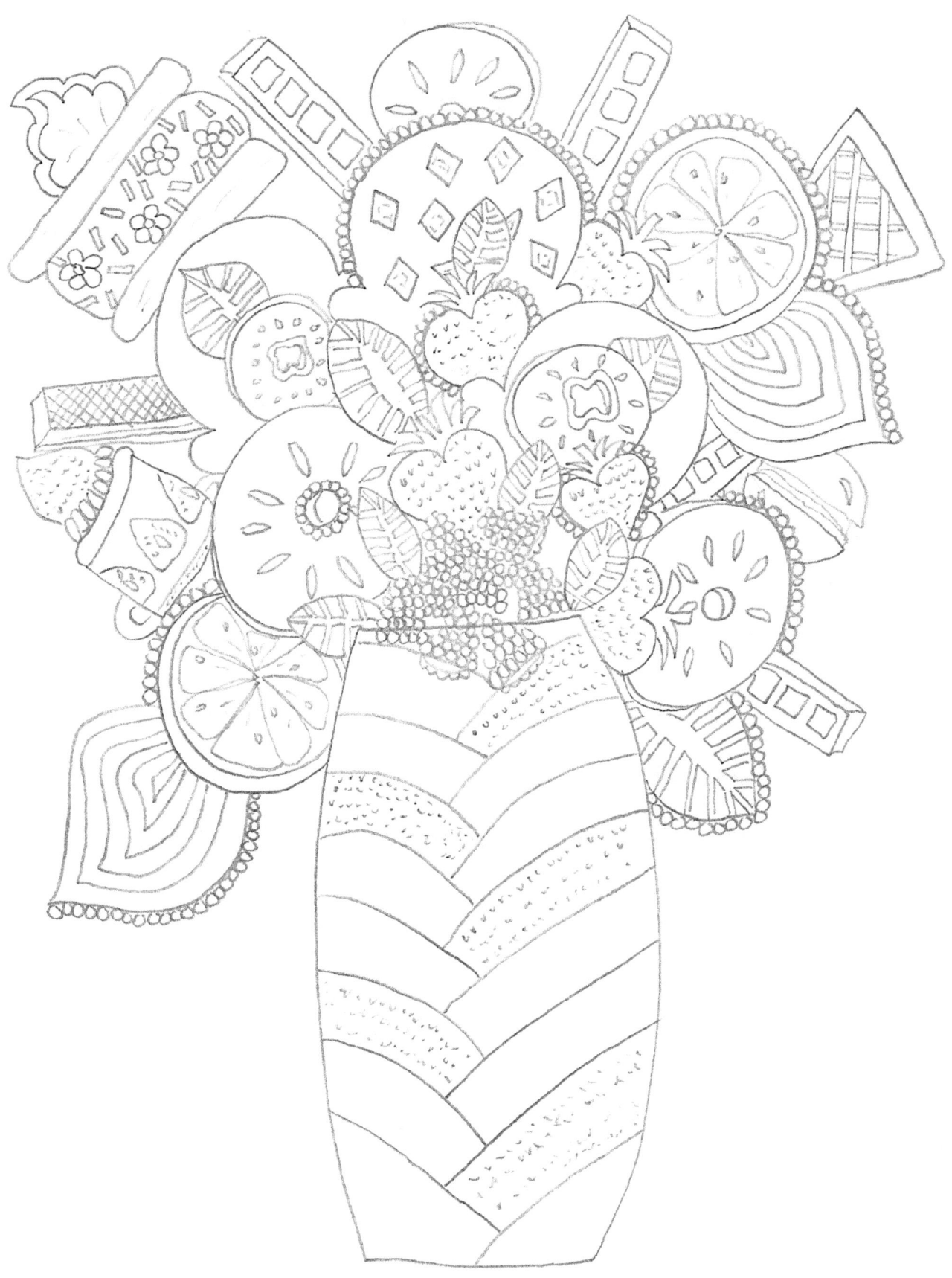

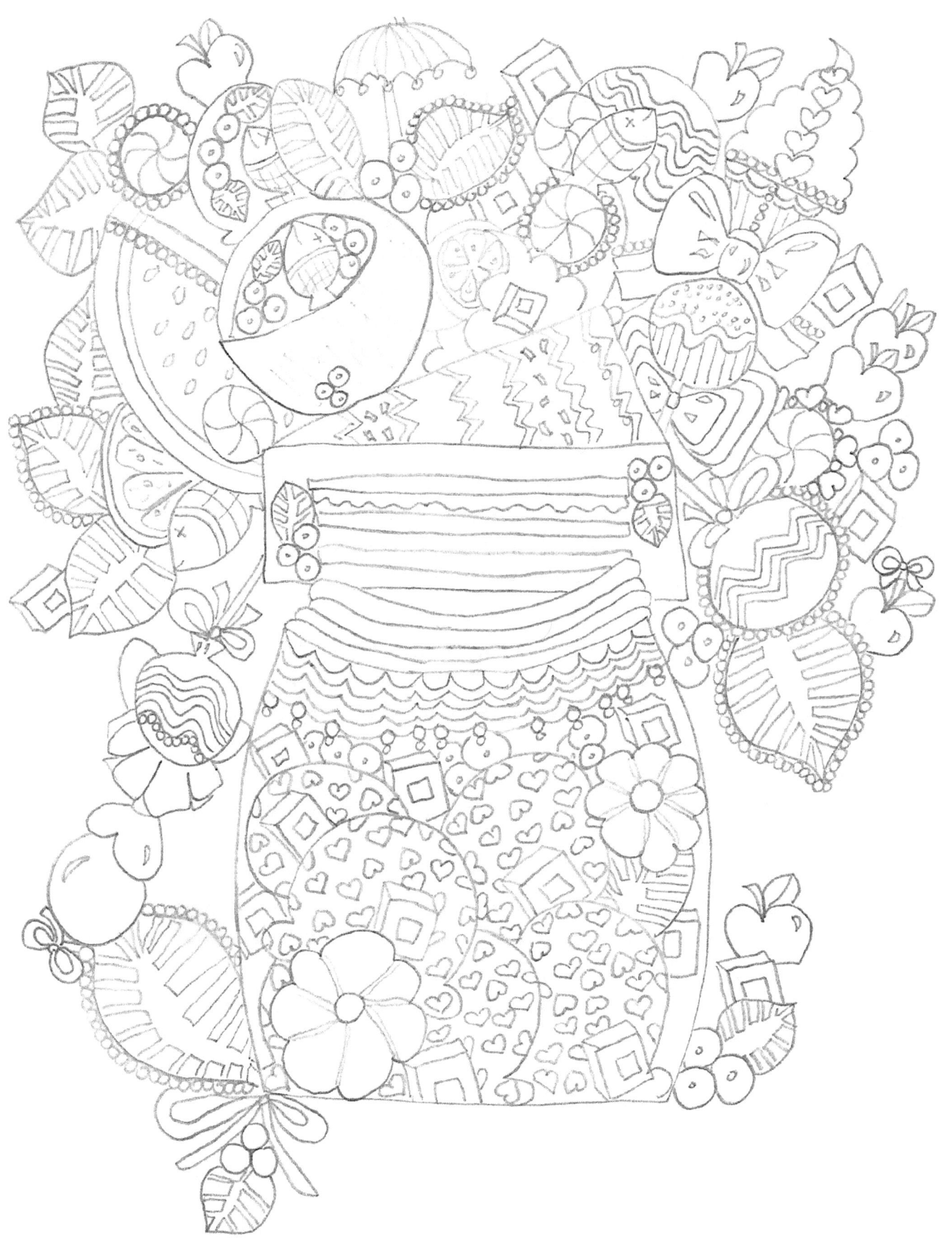

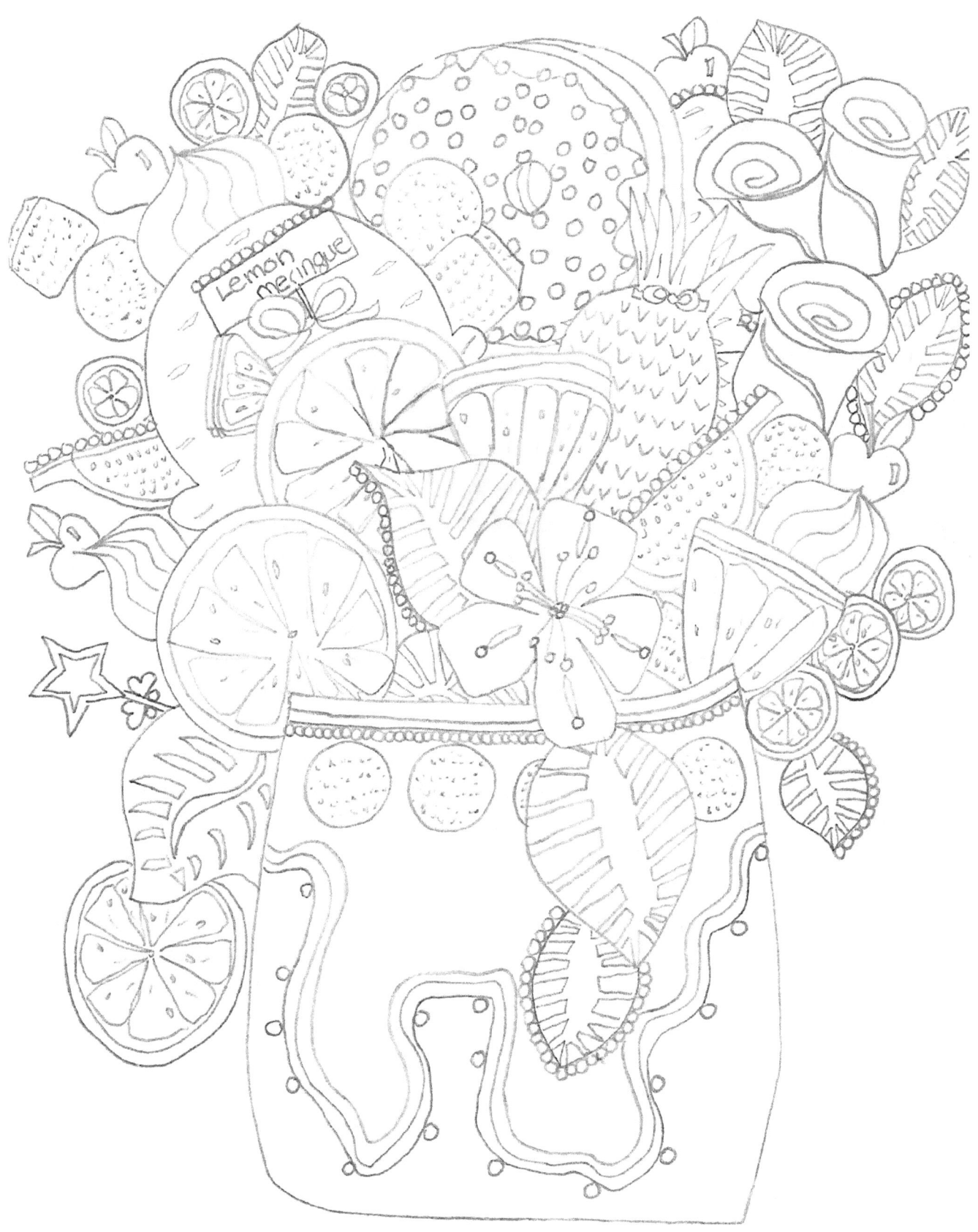

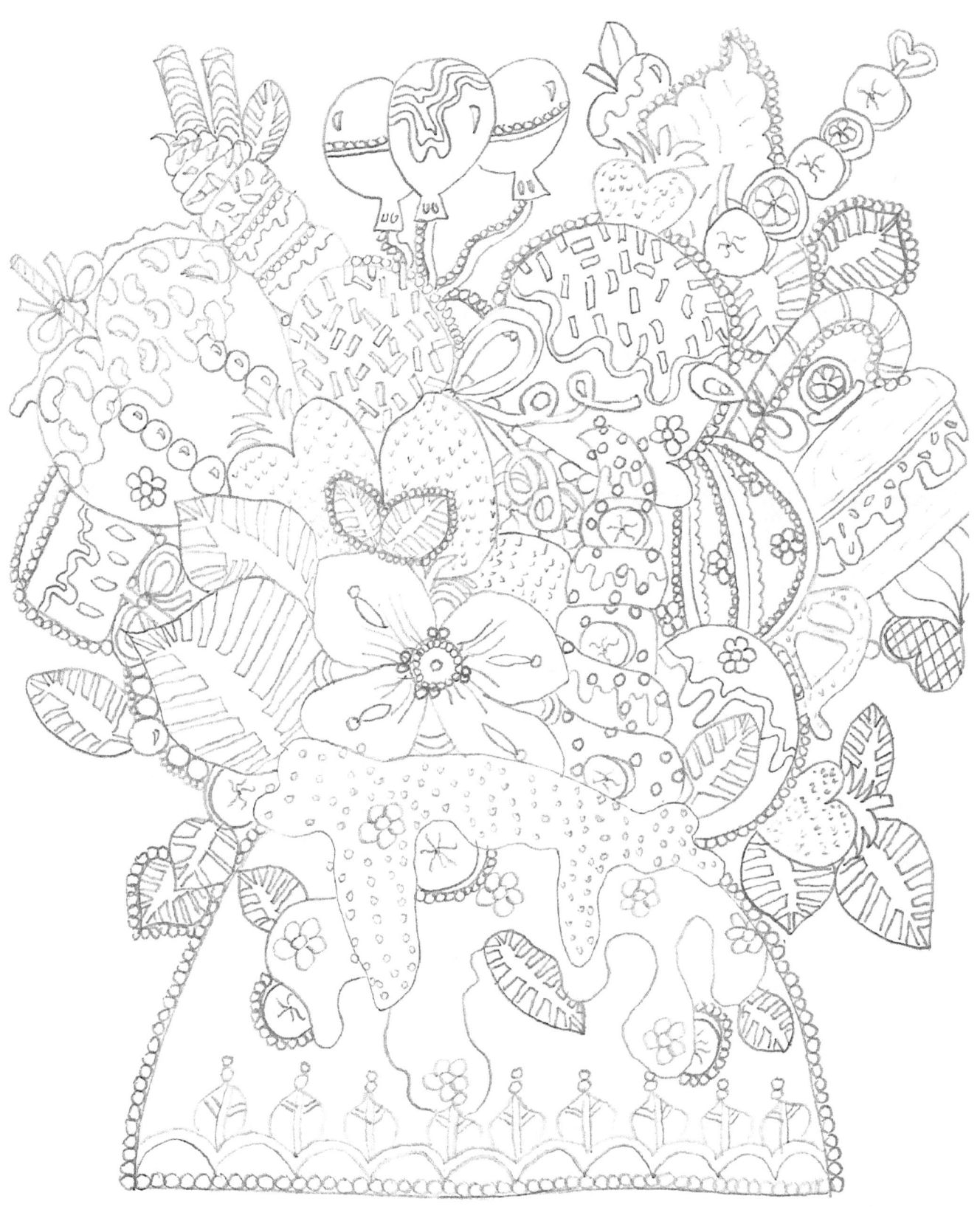

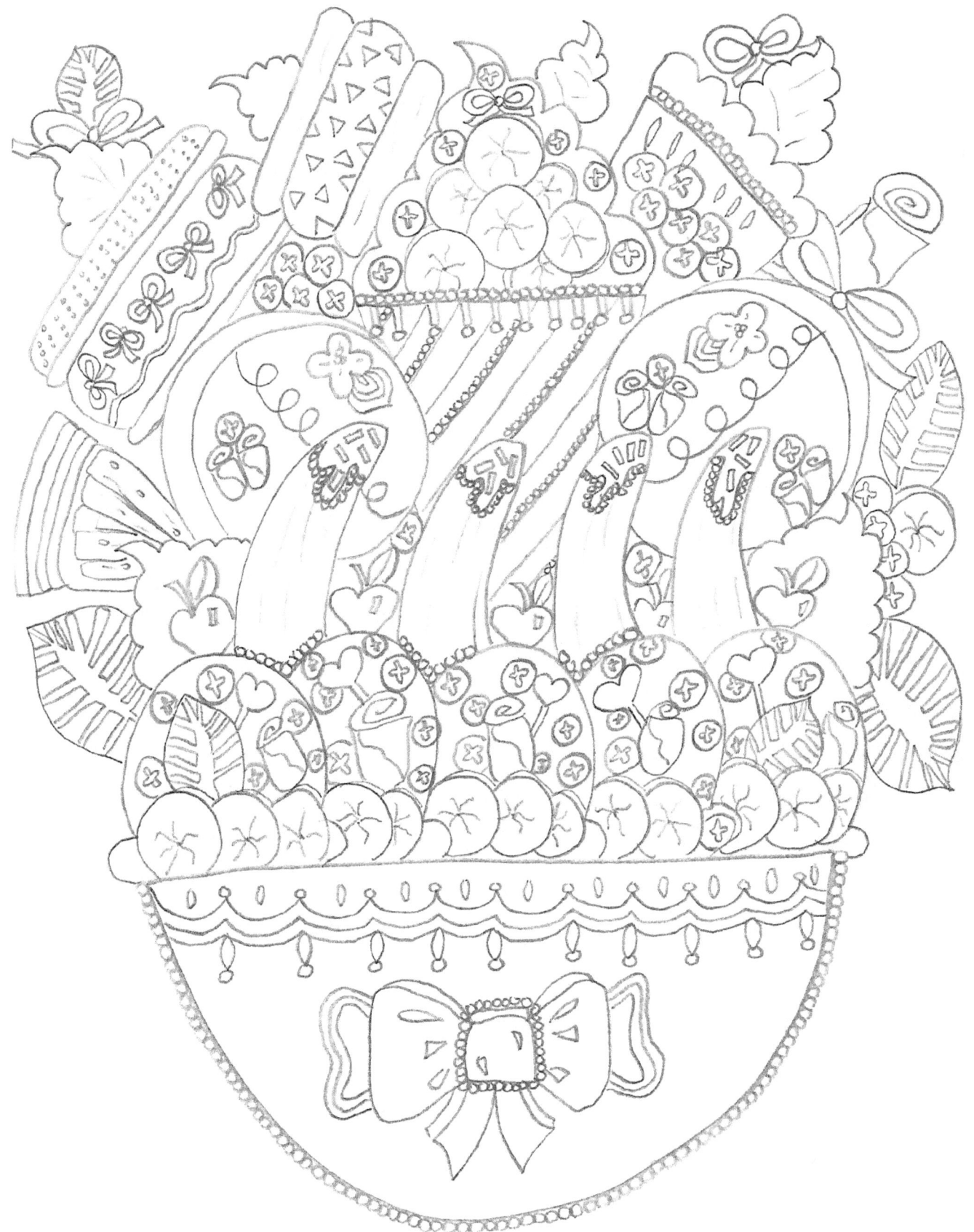

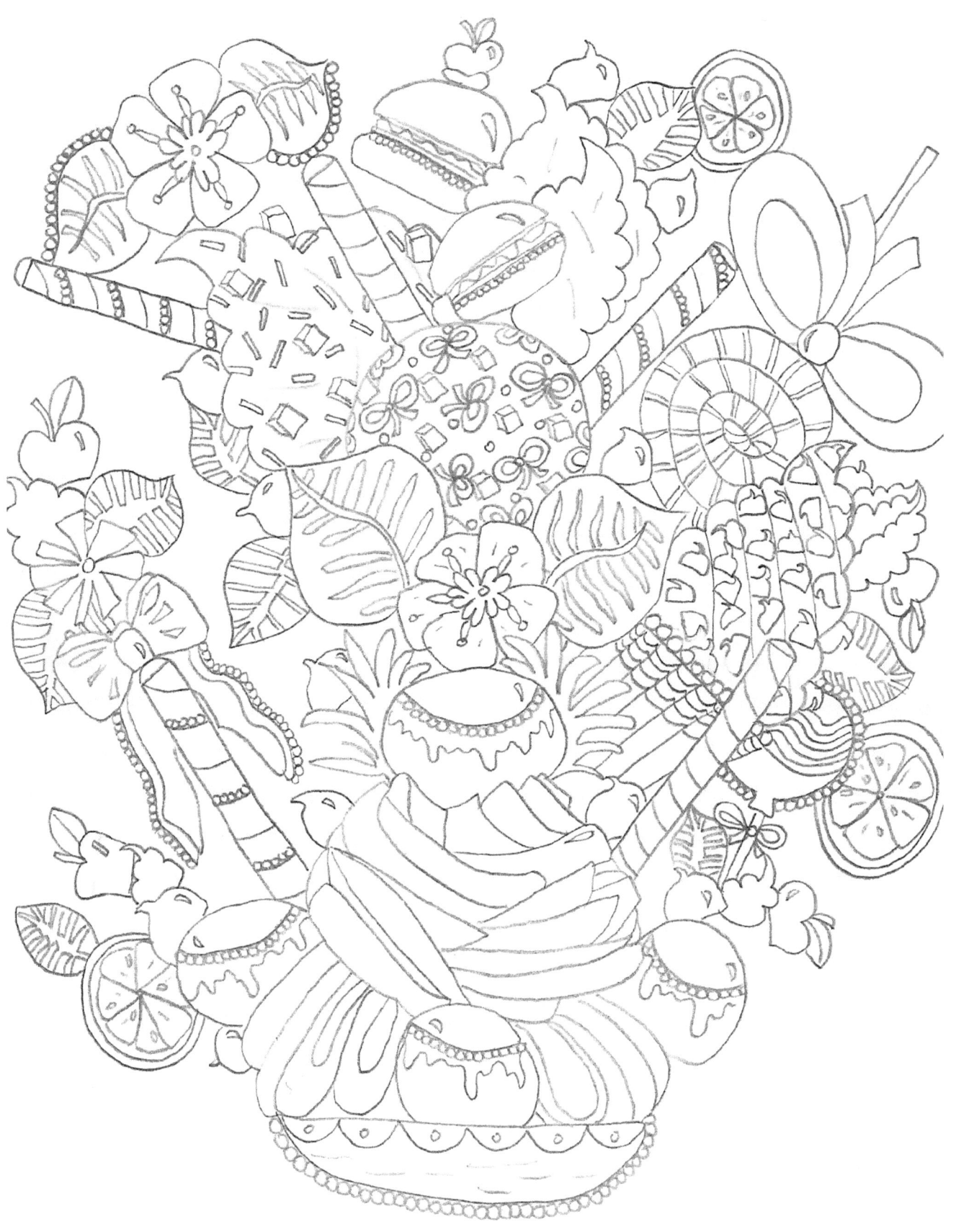

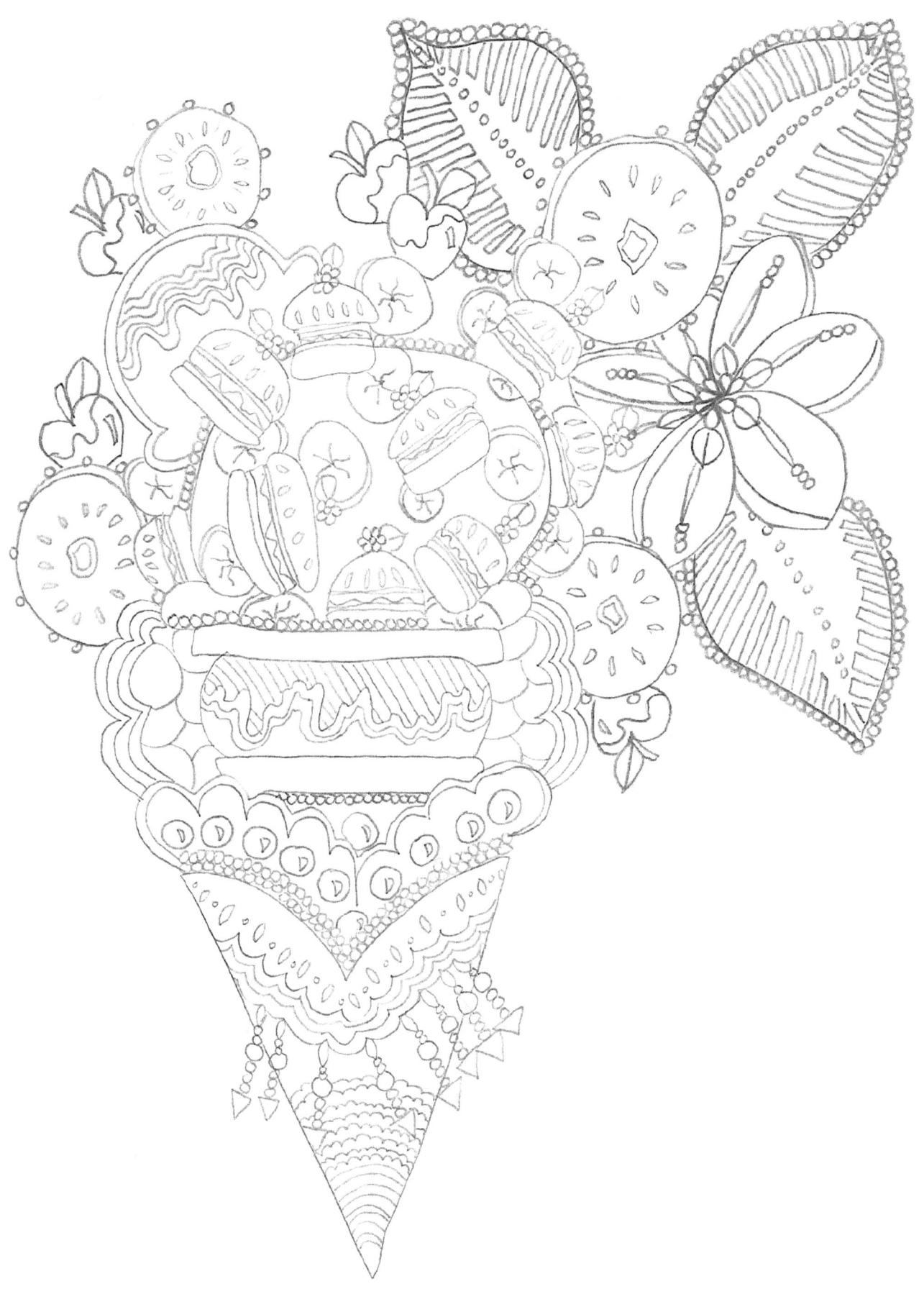

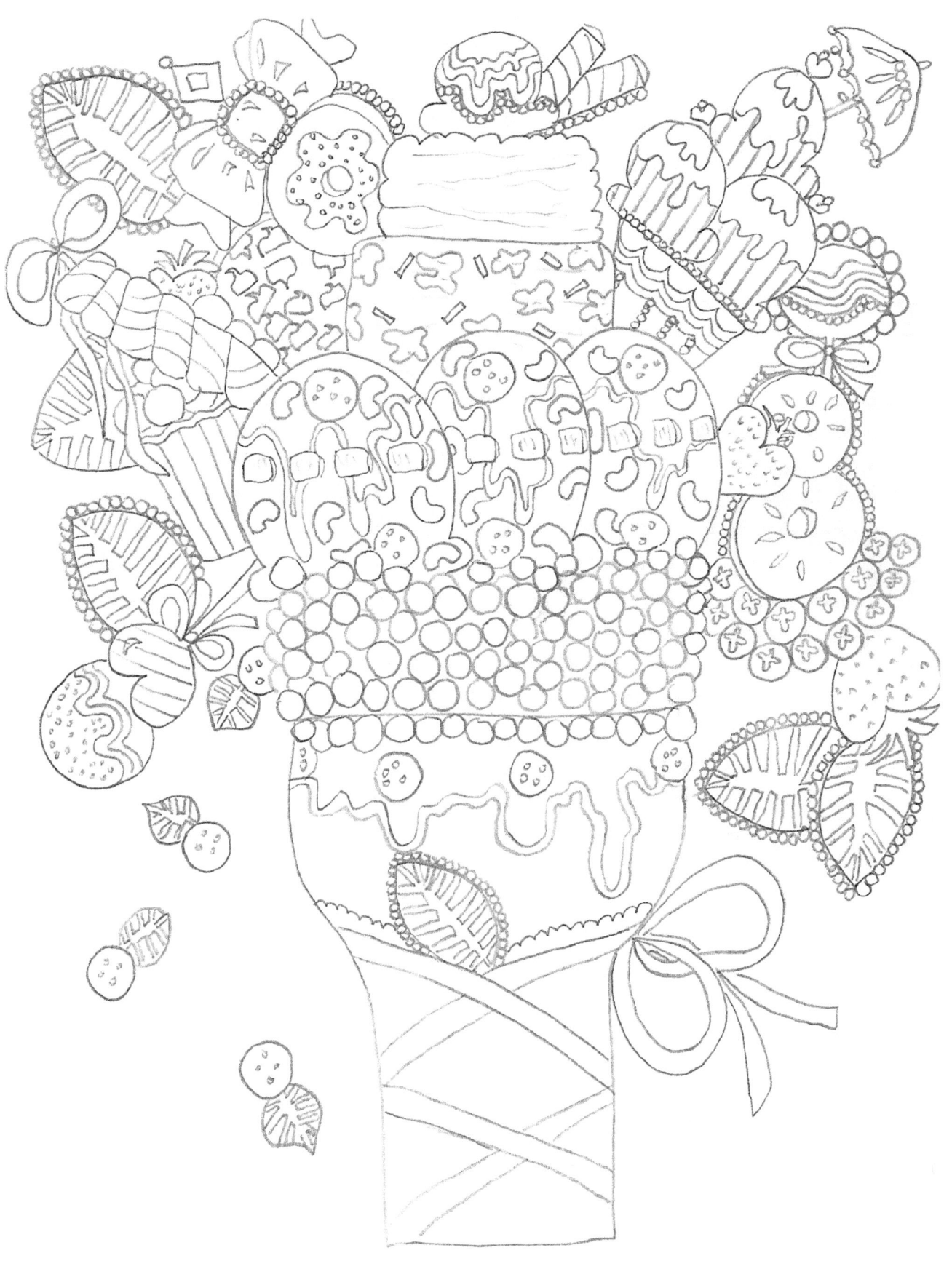

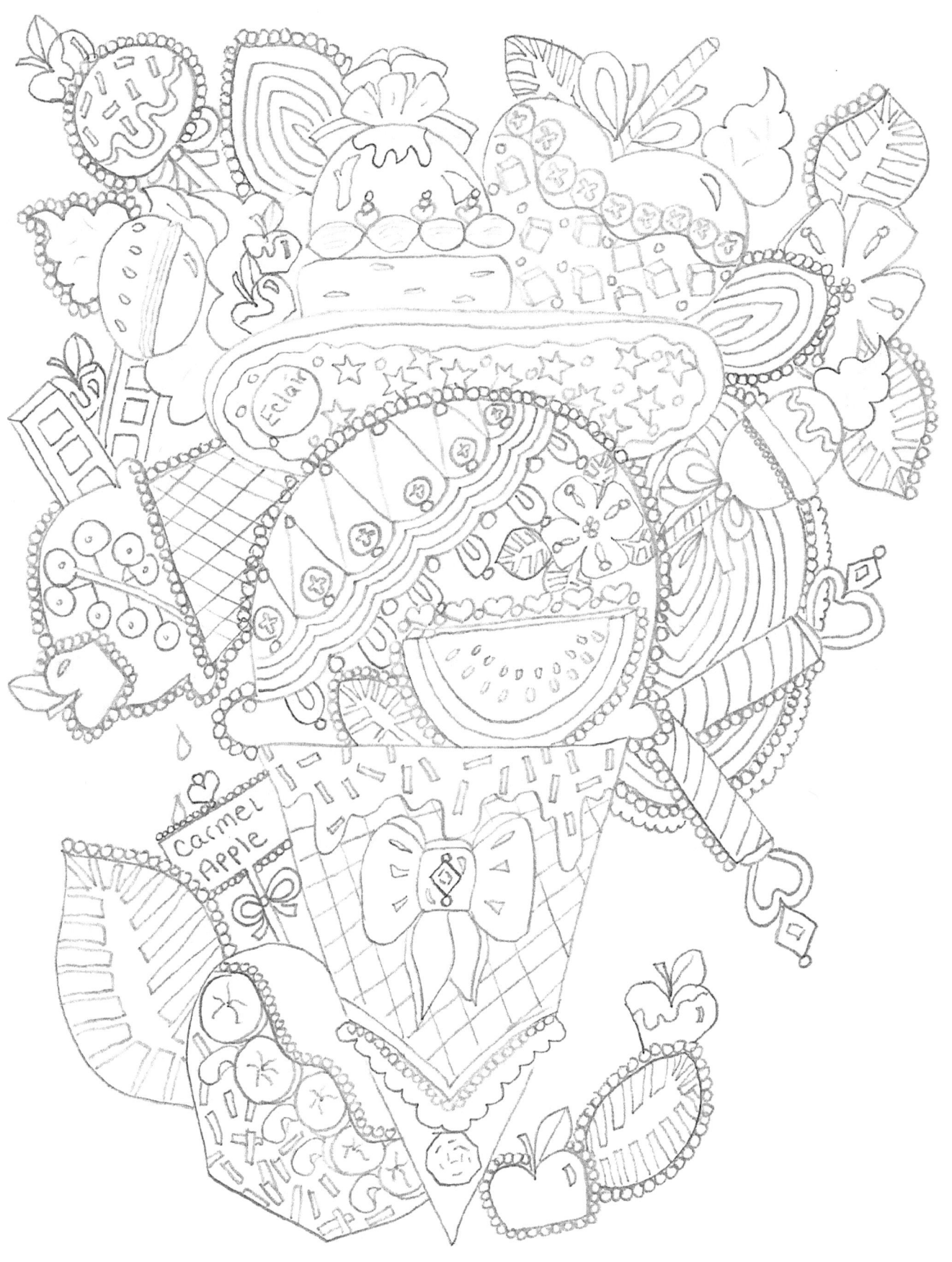

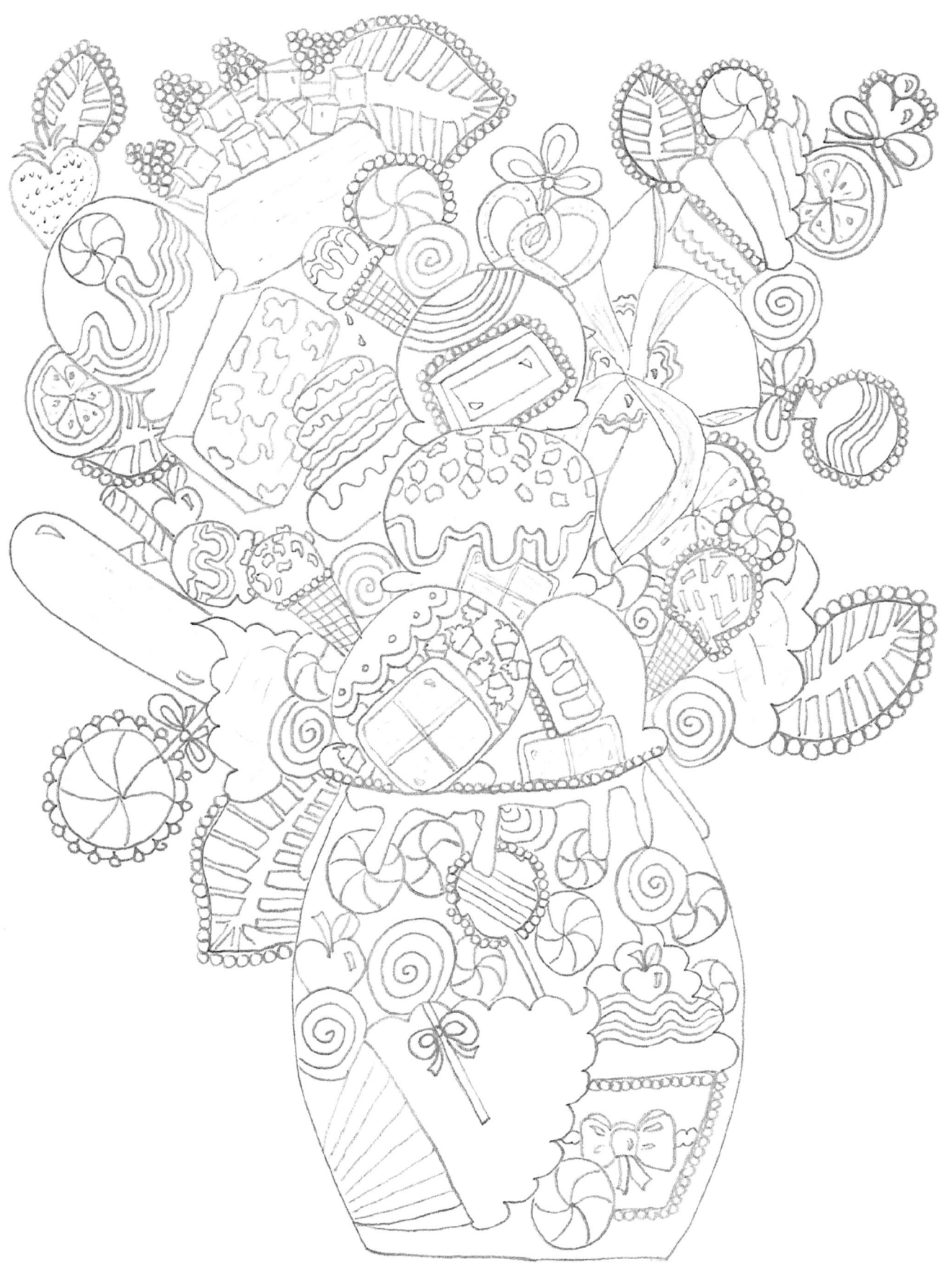

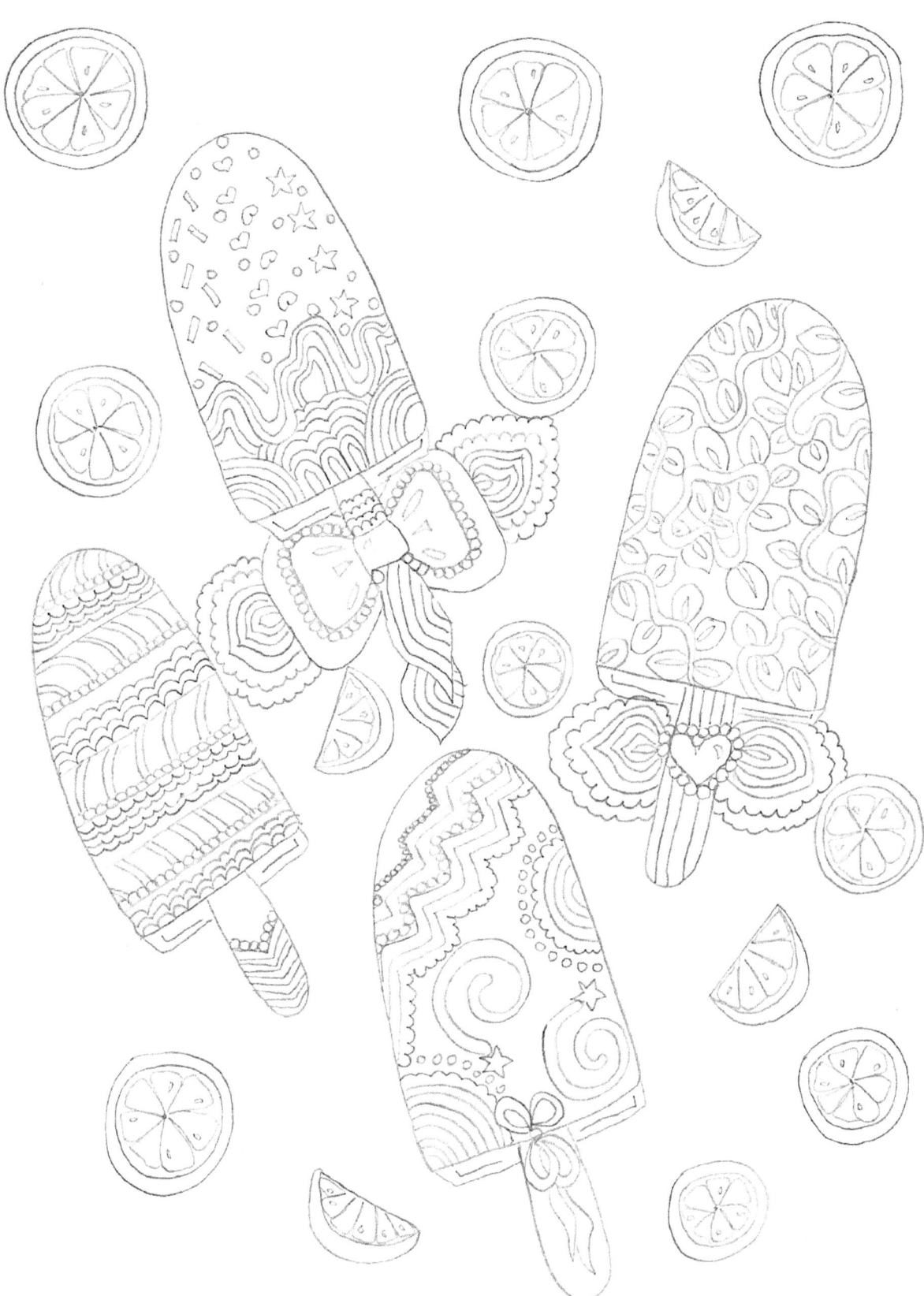

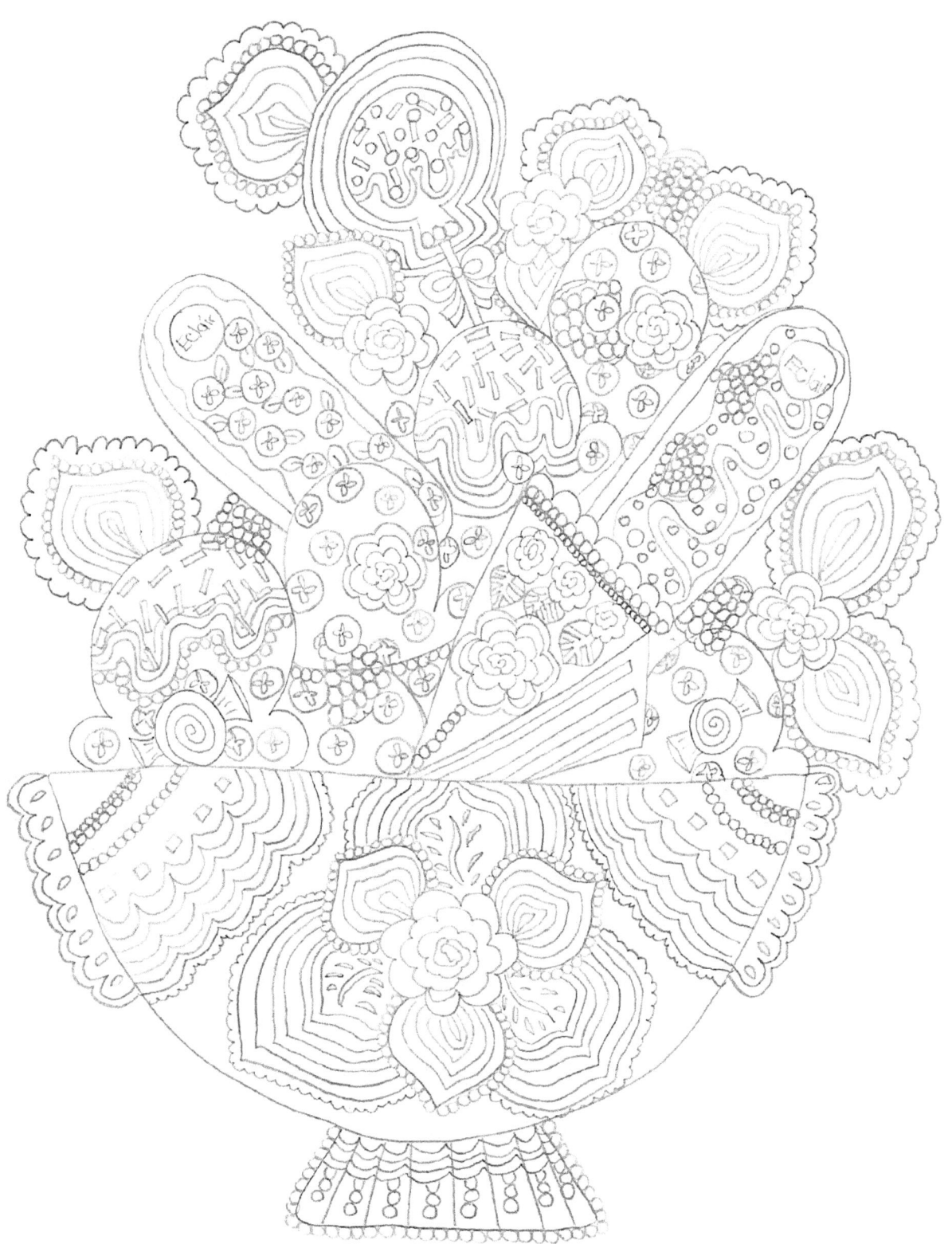

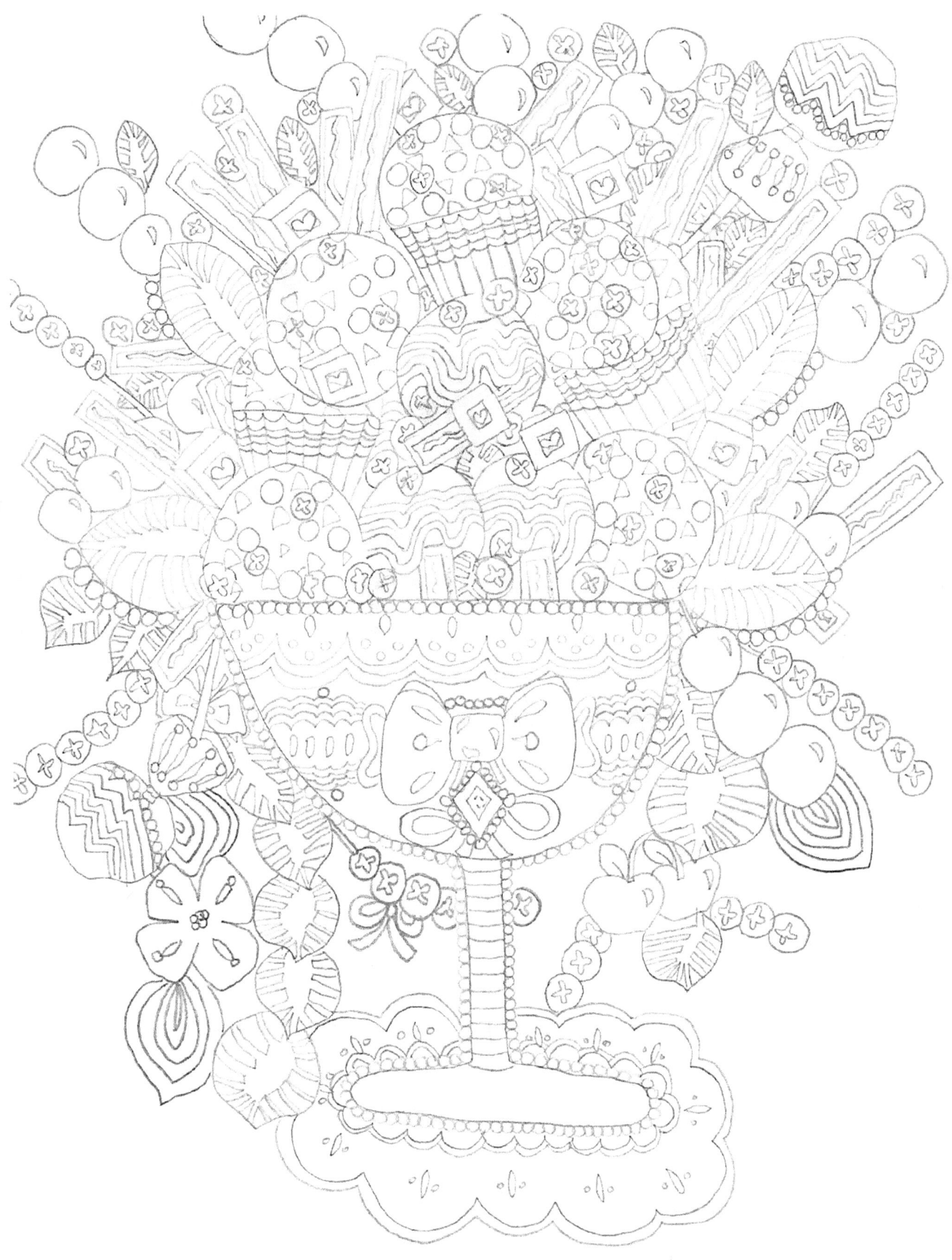

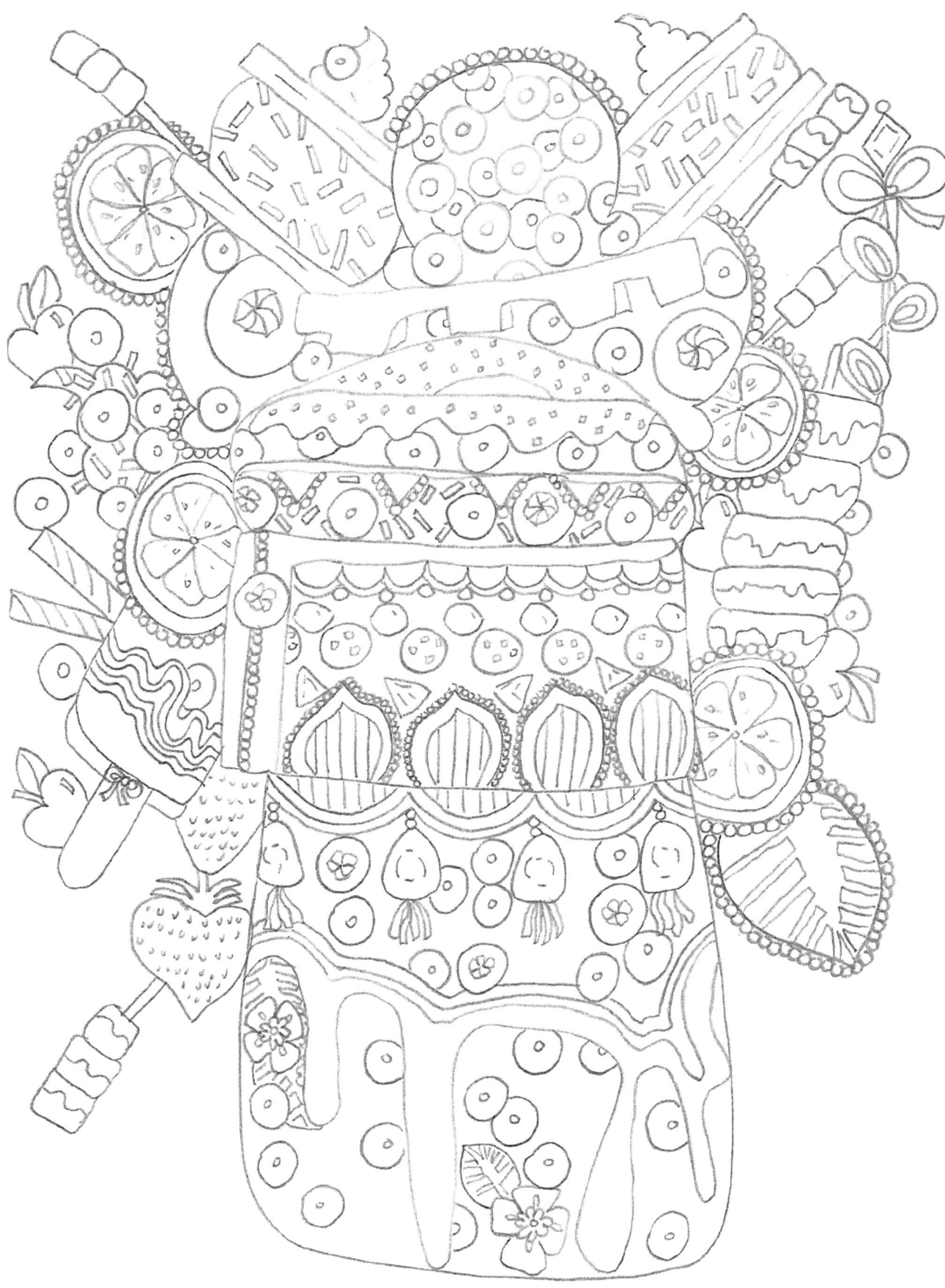

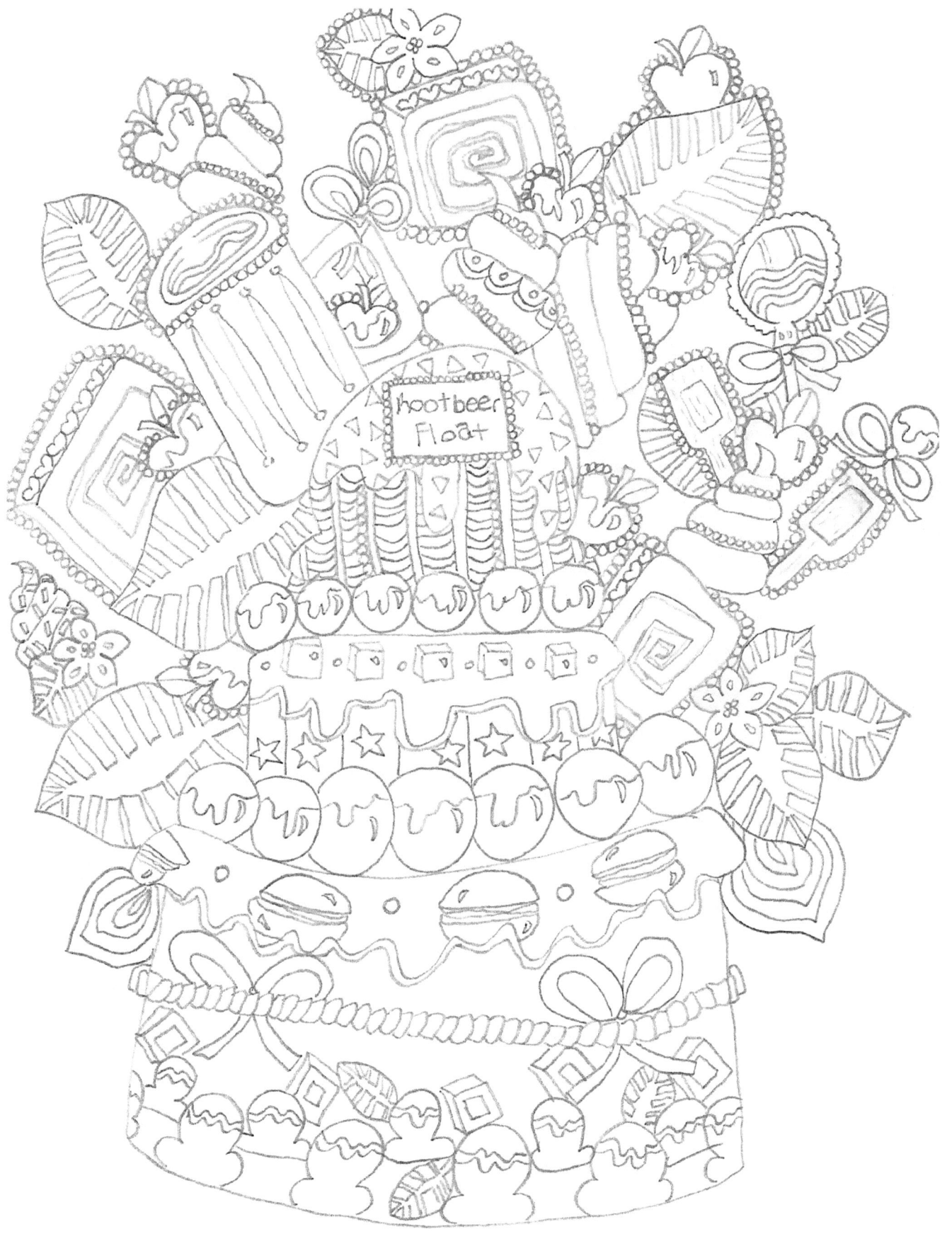

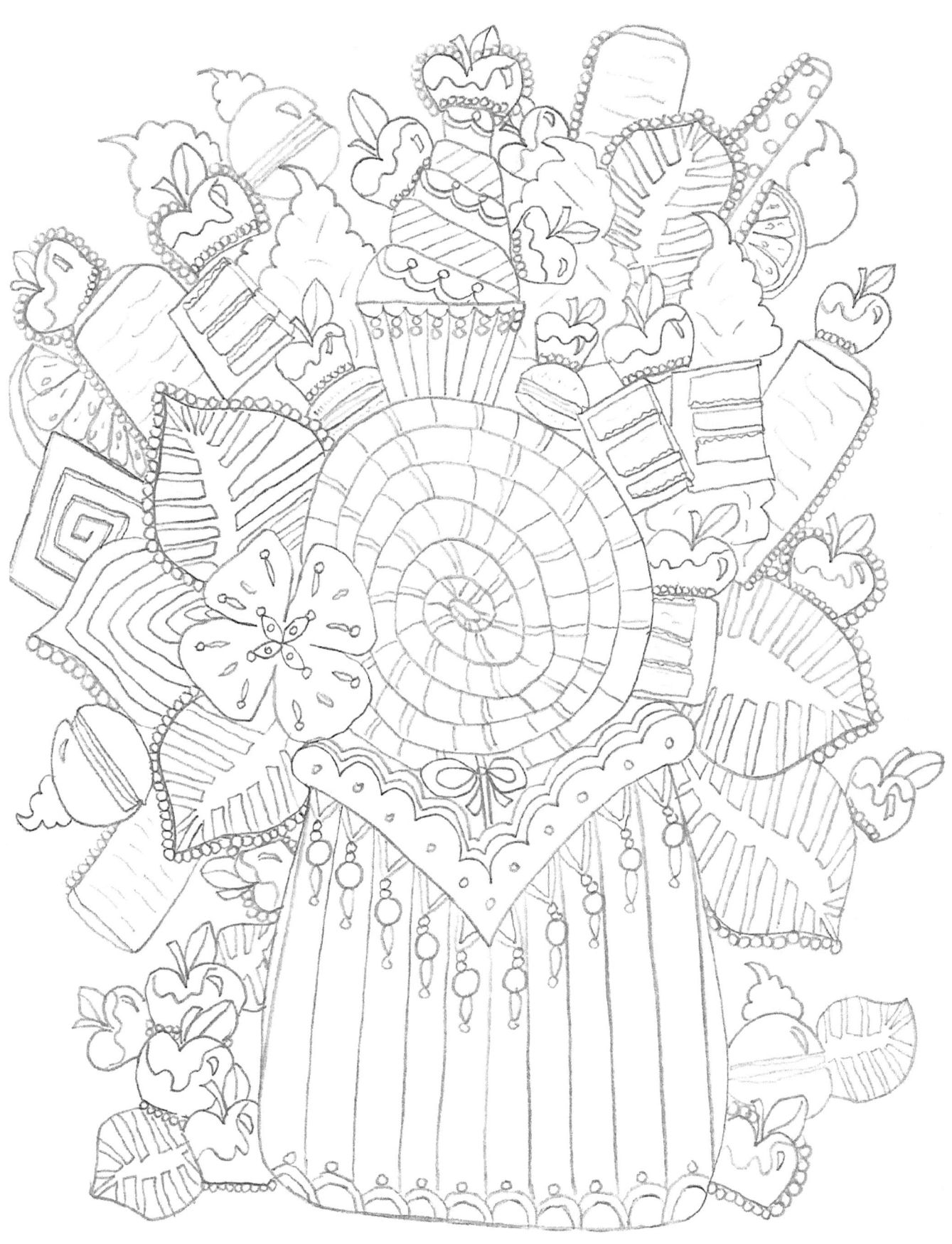

www.ingramcontent.com/pod-product-compliance
Lightning Source LLC
Chambersburg PA
CBHW062334220526
45469CB00008B/2705